Assistive technology
and telecare

"Occupational therapists in social services and healthcare are identified as the 'gatekeepers' for technology *and the authors have not shied away from issues which relate directly to clinical practice: ethics, financial cost/benefits and evidence of effectiveness.* Occupational therapists will be persuaded by the section on the user perspective that it is no small incentive to become knowledgeable about assistive devices. *This book is detailed and offers insights into the broader policy issues which will move practice."*

Sally Fowler Davis, *Principal Lecturer, School of Professional Health Studies, York St John College*

"Thinking the unthinkable does not have to mean thinking the unpalatable. The authors ask whether technology can provide an acceptable and effective means for the community-based delivery of health and social care. Based on their research they arrive at the view that not only is telecare and telemedicine acceptable to patients and users, but it has the potential to save money and improve care and quality of life. *Whether you are new to the field of telehealth or an expert, this book will have something for you.* Starting with a thorough introduction to telecare and the political and social basis for development of telehealth, the report then moves to examine user needs and concerns before considering the functionality of future telehealth systems. Finally, it provides an excellent attempt to model the resource impacts of the introduction of telecare across health, housing and social services. The book acknowledges that this assumes that health, social care and housing professionals are willing to work together to address the needs of individuals in a holistic fashion and this, rather than technology, is the real challenge for the future."

John Hennock, *Executive Director, Association of Social Alarm Providers (the UK association for telecare)*

"The joint health and social care agenda is the major challenge facing the caring services in the 21st century. Assistive technologies, eHealth and telecare systems promise to revolutionise the scope and scale of assistive care. The challenges that eHealth poses for service re-engineering will be the focus of service development for the next decade and *this report not only describes the present system and technology, but sheds considerable light on future developments and how services and technologies could be delivered in the future. The report is equally of interest to someone new to the field or the expert."*

Dr Nicholas Robinson, *National Clinical Adviser for telemedicine and eHealth (NHS Direct)*

"The evidence for the cost benefit of telecare and assistive technology systems in the UK has, before now, not been readily available. *This publication demonstrates how individual economic, health and social gains can be achieved using such technology.* However, it will also require a better understanding of the needs of older and vulnerable people and a knowledge of how telecare and assistive technology can enhance people's quality of life.

Major new government policies such as Supporting People and the National Service Framework for Older People are beginning to shape this. And *this publication makes a valuable contribution by demonstrating how policy makers, practitioners and industry can meet the government's agenda* and really put policy into practice using telecare and assistive technologies. *Above all, it places people first. The case has now been made."*

David Walden, *Director of Health Services Development, Anchor Trust*

"In much of the industrialised world the proportion of elderly people is increasing. They are living for longer and represent an increasing demand on the healthcare system. Understandably, most elderly people prefer to remain in their own homes for as long as possible. The use of computing and telecommunications to deliver care at a distance is a promising method of addressing the increasing resource demands. *This book draws together the evidence for the benefits of telecare systems and makes a powerful case for their introduction on a wide scale.* As the authors point out, how cost-effective telecare may prove to be is a fundamental question that has yet to be answered. Without the introduction and evaluation of telecare systems, we will never know the answer. *As a source of information for healthcare planners and policy makers, this book will be invaluable."*

Professor Richard Wootton, *Centre for Online Health, University of Queensland, and Editor of the international Journal of Telemedicine and Telecare*

Assistive technology and telecare

Forging solutions for independent living

Simon Brownsell and David Bradley

Edited by Jeremy Porteus

Barnsley District General Hospital **NHS**
NHS Trust

First published in Great Britain in January 2003 by

The Policy Press
34 Tyndall's Park Road
Bristol BS8 1PY
UK

Tel +44 (0)117 954 6800
Fax +44 (0)117 973 7308
e-mail tpp-info@bristol.ac.uk
www.policypress.org.uk

British Library Cataloguing in Publication Data

A catalogue record for this book is available from the British Library

ISBN 1 86134 462 7

Simon Brownsell is a Research Fellow at Barnsley District General Hospital, and an Honorary Research Fellow at the University of Sheffield. **David Bradley** is Professor of Mechatronic Systems at the University of Abertay Dundee.

Cover design by Qube Design Associates, Bristol.

Printed and bound in Great Britain by Hobbs the Printers Ltd, Southampton.

Contents

Foreword

Governments around the world are waking up to the consequences of an ageing population. Issues such as older people's care, health and housing are moving up the social and political agenda. Everywhere there are debates about the best and most cost-effective ways to provide these services.

Meanwhile, there has been the rapid and inexorable advance of information and communications technologies (ICTs), including the emergence of assistive technology and telecare. From humble beginnings – some sheltered housing tenants ringing a bell in a warden's home in 1948 – it is now possible for these technologies to help older people live healthier, safer and more independent lives. They could revolutionise the delivery of health and social care to older people.

But policy makers face difficult questions. Are these technologies cost-effective? Will consumers accept them? Where and how are they best used? Accurate and credible information is required to make difficult decisions on how to take the new technologies forward.

This report provides exactly such information. It not only explains the nature of these innovations, but also addresses the technical, financial and some of the ethical questions they raise. Most importantly, through its conclusions and recommendations, it charts a way forward.

It is time for assistive technology and telecare to enter the mainstream of public policy affecting older people. The sooner policy makers and service providers recognise this, the better. I am confident this report will speed that recognition considerably.

John Belcher, *Chief Executive, Anchor Trust*

Preface

The material in this report is largely derived from research work carried out by Simon Brownsell, for which he was awarded his PhD from the University of Abertay Dundee in 2001. However, a broader context has been added to this material, together with new significant contributions by Jeremy Porteus, drawing on his particular expertise and knowledge of the development of health policy in the UK, and by Mark Hawley, based on his work on service provision.

The motivation for the report derived from the realisation that there was a significant degree of confusion, and indeed misunderstanding, of the possible role of assistive technology and telecare as part of the healthcare structure within the UK, and of the types of technology that could and should be deployed. It was also clear that there was no significant study of the cost implications of introducing an advanced, technology-based telecare system, or of the changes to the current operation and practice of healthcare within the UK for a telecare strategy to be cost-effective. The report therefore begins by setting out to provide a context within which assistive technology and telecare provision in the UK, and indeed elsewhere, can be developed.

Following this, it then considers the evidence for the introduction of advanced assistive technologies and telecare systems and provides a cost model for such a system. In presenting this model, it must be emphasised, however, that it is aimed at identifying the *degree* and *type* of change that needs to take place, for instance, with regard to reducing the time spent in hospital by older people or delaying their entry into care, and *does not* suggest any definitive link

between the introduction of such an advanced system and the achievement of such changes.

Finally, the report considers the implications of the introduction of advanced assistive technologies and telecare on healthcare provision and puts forward recommendations as to the way forward. The structure of the report is as follows:

As society ages, greater demands will be made on health, care and support mechanisms. Chapter 1 introduces the reasons why technology is being investigated as a possible solution. In Chapter 2, the current community alarm system is described, along with definitions of appropriate home-based technologies. In particular, telecare, telemedicine and smart homes are introduced, with examples of previous developments and current research. In order for telecare to flourish it is necessary that policy supports the refocusing of resources that telecare suggests. Current housing, health and social service policies are reviewed in Chapter 3, while attention is also given to policies that are under development. Telecare is a new and emerging discipline and Chapter 4 therefore indicates where telecare could be positioned in relation to present health, care and support mechanisms. Potential user groups and types of telecare provision are also highlighted.

The second section to the report looks at the evidence. Community alarm users are currently the largest group of telecare equipment users and Chapter 5 reports on possibly the largest face-to-face survey of their views regarding future telecare equipment. In the UK, the views of potential telecare users are investigated, while the perspectives of the warden and community alarm control centre

operator are also included. Based on the views of
users and providers and a review of current
technology trends, the components of telecare
systems for the coming years are defined in Chapter
6. Particular attention is given to the second
generation system, and it is suggested that such a
system could be in place by 2003-05. Perhaps one of
the greatest stumbling blocks to the widespread
introduction of telecare services is that little is known
of the funding issues. Based on a comprehensive cost
analysis model, Chapter 7 indicates that the second
generation telecare system, defined in Chapter 6, has
the potential to require less overall funding than the
present system.

The third section looks at the implications for
telecare, and makes some recommendations. The
introduction of second and subsequent generations of
telecare will inevitably change the way in which the
community alarm control centres function, and a
model has been created that simulates the possible
impact. Based on this model, anticipated changes to
the workload can be investigated to ascertain whether
telecare can be delivered with the present resources
(see Chapter 8). Possible implications are highlighted
in Chapter 9 in a number of areas, such as general
practice, organisational structure, human resources,
and intermediate care. While it is difficult to predict
the future, an attempt has been made to indicate the
kind of changes that are likely to result from the
widespread introduction of assistive technology and
telecare, and the greater use of information and
communications technologies (ICTs). Chapter 10
provides a summary of previous chapters, and
concludes by putting forward some key
recommendations that various organisations and
individuals need to embrace if telecare is to continue
to progress and to be a welcome component of
service delivery in the future.

Acknowledgements

Simon Brownsell and David Bradley would like to acknowledge the support of Pentyre plc, Attendo Systems and HET Software for their funding of the research study on which parts of the report are based.

Special thanks are due to Jeremy Porteus and Mark Hawley for their valuable contributions and for reviewing early drafts of the report. However, the responsibility for the completed version rests solely with the authors and the views expressed do not necessarily represent those of the University of Abertay Dundee, Anchor Trust or Barnsley District General Hospital.

Others have contributed through discussions and by commenting on the work as it developed. In particular, Gareth Williams, Sharon Levy, Katja Huebbers and Graham Brownsell deserve special mention.

Finally, we are particularly grateful for the support of Anchor Trust in sponsoring this report, and for their continued commitment to the development of systems and services for the benefit of older people.

About the authors

Dr Simon Brownsell completed his PhD at the University of Abertay Dundee in 2001 and at the time of publication is a Research Fellow at Barnsley District General Hospital and an Honorary Research Fellow at the University of Sheffield, where he is involved in various aspects of assistive technology. He has an interest in all aspects of assistive technology and telecare and his current work centres around the development and evaluation of technology to assist independent living. Specific areas of activity include the development of automatic speech recognition systems for people with speech impairments, mobile phone navigation for older people and smart home technology. He is the author or co-author of a number of research and general interest papers on assistive technology and telecare and, with Jeremy Porteus, the co-author of the Anchor Trust/Housing Corporation telecare book on life-style monitoring.

David Bradley is Professor of Mechatronic Systems at the University of Abertay Dundee where he is responsible for a number of projects in the area of assistive technology and telecare. He is particularly interested in the systems definition level, definition of intelligent systems such as those required by assistive technology and telecare, and of the ways in which machine-based intelligence can be used as part of a telecare programme. Current research includes the 'Telecare in Tayside' project, which is looking at the way in which users respond to different levels of technology provision, and which is working towards the development of a needs-led methodology for matching assistive technology to client need and a project to develop an intelligent exoskeleton to support the rehabilitation process. He is the author or co-author of five textbooks and over 100 articles in journals and at conferences.

Jeremy Porteus formerly managed the Corporate Policy Team in the Chief Executive's Unit at Anchor Trust. Jeremy is on the Office of the Deputy Prime Minister's Housing for Older People Working Group. He is well placed to represent the views and experiences of older people and help put policy into practice. He is the joint author of *Using telecare: Exploring technologies for independent living for older people* (2000) and has commissioned major research projects on the housing and support needs of older people, and also contributed to other publications including *Lifetime housing in Europe* (2001). He has also visited the Far East on several occasions for the Department of Trade and Industry to investigate the development of telecare and smart housing solutions for older people and for people with disabilities.

Prior to joining Anchor in 1997, Jeremy worked for the Royal National Institute for the Blind and helped influence national and local policy on housing management and building design issues for people with a visual impairment. Jeremy is a Committee Member of Care & Repair England, a national charity supporting older and disabled people to make improvements to their housing circumstances. He is also a member of the Committee and Advisory Group for the post-graduate programme on Inclusive Environments at Reading University.

Professor Mark Hawley is Consultant Clinical Scientist and Director of Research and Development at Barnsley District General Hospital NHS Trust. Mark has over 10 years' experience of assessing and providing assistive technology to assist older and disabled people to live independently in their own homes. He currently leads the research programme of the hospital with particular emphasis on developing assistive technology to enable people to live independently. He also leads the Sheffield Institute for Studies in Ageing (SISA) research theme on 'New Technology for Old Age' at the University of Sheffield, where he is Visiting Professor.

Contact details

Simon Brownsell
simon.brownsell@bdgh-tr.trent.nhs.uk
David Bradley
d.bradley@tay.ac.uk
Jeremy Porteus
porteus.beech@btinternet.com
Mark Hawley
mark.hawley@bdgh-tr.trent.nhs.uk

Section 1
The need for assistive technology and telecare

1

The need for assistive technology and telecare

Simon Brownsell and David Bradley

... we envisage that the first point of contact with health care will be through a 'virtual' cyber-physician (CP)[1]. Accessed through a TV screen, the CP will replace other forms of triage[2] such as the telephone and give access to information about professionals, hospitals and other aspects of health care. Access to part or all of the user's health biography would require use of smart card or a biological identifier such as retinal vessels. (DTI, 2000, p 18)

This is the projected view of healthcare in 2020 as expressed by a DTI panel of experts (2000). They predict that a patient's first point of contact with their doctor will be through a television screen, and that identification of the user may be performed automatically, for instance by recognising them by the unique parameters of their eye or other means. Clearly a considerable change from today's interaction with a general practitioner (GP).

The use of technology in the delivery of healthcare has been widespread in hospitals for many years and has had a significant positive impact on the diagnosis and treatment of many conditions. The personal computer crept almost unnoticed into GP surgeries and may now be considered as standard equipment for the GP to generate prescriptions, retrieve personal data, and increasingly to access information on the NHS network and Internet. While technological developments have continued in hospitals, and arguably in the medical profession as a whole, healthcare developments for the home have not been so forthcoming. However, over recent years interest in telecare has grown considerably, with telecare being defined as:

> The remote or enhanced delivery of health and social care services to people in their own home by means of telecommunications and computer-based systems. (Barnes et al, 1998, p 169)

Through the use of technology, telecare seeks to deliver, and allow access to, health, care and support mechanisms for people living in their own homes. There are several reasons why telecare is increasingly being viewed with greater interest.

Current levels of support and care

There is evidence to suggest that the current arrangements do not provide adequate levels of care. During the 1980s, low level preventive services such as Meals on Wheels or home care support became more "thinly spread" (Parry and Thompson, 1993, p 12). This continued in the 1990s with the Association of Directors of Social Services and the Local Government Association suggesting that home care and residential care faced cutbacks as social services departments faced an average 3.4% shortfall in the 1998 budget (BBC News, 1998a). This has culminated in a more intensive service, where greater amounts of assistance are provided to a smaller number of people. By way of illustration, between

---

[1] The physician (doctor or nurse) may assist the patient without being in the room with them; they can see and hear the patient through a computer or television screen instead.

[2] A process of sorting people into groups based on their need or likely benefit from immediate medical treatment.

1992 and 1996, while the total number of home care hours increased by 50%, there was a reduction of around 7% in the number of households receiving the service. The resulting change in focus has been reflected with a change in name, from the original 'home help' to the now more commonly used term 'home care' (Godfrey, 1999, pp 11-13).

The 1994 General Household Survey (GHS) observed that the predominant users of domiciliary services were those aged 75 and over, primarily women and people living alone (OPCS, 1996). Focusing purely on home care in the UK indicates that in 1996, 83% of the recipients were aged 65 and over, with 64% of these aged 75 and over (DoH *Statistical Bulletin*, 1998). In terms of assisting people who live on their own, it has been suggested that local authorities are six times more likely to help people in single occupant dwellings (Goldring, 1998). It can therefore be concluded that older people living alone are the main beneficiaries of 'care'.

A growing number of older people

A fundamental question of importance to the development of telecare is the question of whether there will be a need to provide additional care in the future. From the above it is clear that older people are the main recipients of care and that currently there are some difficulties delivering care to all who would once have qualified for assistance. If the user base, the number of older people, increases, then the

available services will be 'stretched' even further. Figures from the House of Commons Health Committee, and echoed by the Department of Health, suggest that 5.1% of the population is currently aged between 75 to 84, with 1.7% aged 85 and over. By 2021 it is suggested that these figures will have increased to 6.2% and 2.3% respectively (DoH, 1996). Possible demographic changes for the UK are summarised in Table 1.1 (Ermisch, 1990).

Table 1.1 highlights the dependency ratio, defined as the ratio of people of working age compared to non-working age groups (0-15 and 65+). Considering the overall dependency ratio, a steady increase can be observed from 55.6% in 1987 to an estimated 64.3% in 2027. At present, care provision in the UK is supported through tax income. With such an increase in the dependency ratio it may be difficult in the future to raise enough income from this source alone.

Due in part to the industrial revolution, demographic ageing began in the UK before many other countries; consequently the growth of the UK's older population has been slower in the past two decades when compared to other western countries (Warnes, 1993). However, the UK is only one among many countries where society is ageing. In the past 50 years within the countries of the European Union, the proportion of persons aged 60 and over has changed from 1 in 14, to 1 in 5. For the last 20 years the average age of the European workforce has been constant at around 40; however, by 2015 it will have

Table 1.1: Changes in the UK population (1987-2027)

	1987	1997	2007	2017	2027
Total population (000s)	**55,355**	**57,062**	**58,110**	**58,869**	**59,616**
% aged					
0-4	6.4	7.0	6.1	6.2	6.3
5-15	13.7	14.3	14.8	13.2	13.6
16-64	64.3	63.0	63.5	63.1	60.9
65-74	8.9	8.4	8.1	10.0	10.3
75+	6.7	7.3	7.5	7.5	8.9
Dependency ratios (%)					
Child (0-15)[a]	31.3	33.8	32.8	30.7	32.7
Elderly (65+)[b]	24.2	25.0	24.6	27.8	31.6
Overall[c]	55.6	58.8	57.4	58.5	64.3

[a] Persons aged 0-15 as percentage of persons aged 16-64.
[b] Persons aged 65 and older as percentage of persons aged 16-64.
[c] The ratio of those aged <16 and >65 to those aged 16-64.
Source: Ermisch (1990)

risen to 42.5 (Gavigan et al, 1999) and it is estimated that by 2020, 1 in 4 persons in Europe will be aged 60 and over (Eurolink Centre for International Research, 1992).

A potential shortage of informal carers?

A carer can been defined as a "… person looking after or providing some form of regular service for a sick, handicapped or elderly person living in their own home or elsewhere" (Green, 1988). Carers may be formal, that is, they are paid to provide care, or informal when no charge is made for their support. Informal carers have historically compensated for any shortfall of formal care provision and in combination with formal care provided greater support to some people. As the number of older people increases, there may be an increasing reliance on informal care to 'bridge' the almost inevitable care gap.

Studies suggest that there are currently between 6 million (Brodie-Smith, 1993) and 6.8 million (OPCS, 1994) informal carers in the UK, predominantly family members, and they cannot be completely relied on to provide long-term care. In financial terms, attempts have been made to cost informal care and estimates for savings range from between £15-24 billion (Brodie-Smith, 1993) to £34 billion (Griffiths, 1996) per annum.

Spouses or partners are the main providers of informal care, followed by children. The number of children a couple have therefore affects the number of potential carers in later life. Over recent decades the family has changed from a 'horizontal' spread, with many children, to a 'vertical' spread, with fewer children but more generations alive. This has been referred to as a transition to a 'beanpole' family (Myers and Coltrane, 1993). The reduction of the age gap between generations observed in recent years may also mean that a grandparent is far from being dependent (Tinker, 1997). Indeed, in a national survey it was found that the grandmother was the second most frequent source of childcare for women in employment, the most frequent being the husband (Martin and Roberts, 1984). As a consequence, there is the potential for care to be provided by both children and grandchildren (Wenger, 1993).

The former UK Department of Health and Social Security (now just the Department of Health) has commented that although family links are irreplaceable, it cannot be assumed that the family can carry the whole responsibility for caring for the growing numbers of very old people. Therefore the wider community may have to provide some of the support traditionally expected of the family (DHSS, 1978). It may be that technology will also have a role to play.

Delivering support where it is needed

The home (or nursing home, sheltered housing and so on) is considered the most likely location in which care is provided, with people needing continuing care preferring to receive this within their own homes (Curry and Norris, 1997). Indeed, 80% of older people want to live and stay in their own homes (DoH, 1992). The 1990 NHS and Community Care Act encourages people to stay in their own homes with additional help if required, yet, as previously suggested, the home care service has become an intensive service offering support to fewer numbers of people. Alber (1993) has suggested that when community services are lacking, then the stress on informal carers increases and consequently an older person reliant on such care may ultimately come to be placed in residential care (Alber, 1993). An undesirable result for all concerned.

The healthcare costs associated with an ageing society

On average, older people in the UK use 3.5 times the amount of hospital care used by those under 65 (Wanless, 2001). Breaking this down into age groups shows that, on average, the annual cost to the NHS of a person aged over 85 is approximately 6 times that of someone aged 16-44, and 4 times that of someone aged 45-64, as evident in Figure 1.1. Because older people tend to have a greater need for health and social services than the young, the bulk of resources are directed to meeting the needs of older people. Consequently, during 1998/99 the NHS spent 40%, and social services nearly 50%, of their budgets on people aged 65 and older (DoH, 2001a).

Figure 1.1: Average annual per capita expenditure on hospital and community health services in England (1996-99)

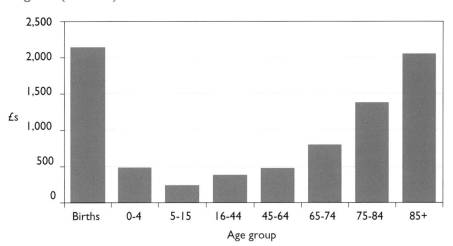

Source: Wanless (2001)

If potential difficulties can be detected earlier than at present, then assistance can be provided as part of a move from a reactive to a preventative system that should result in a reduction in per capita healthcare costs (DoH, 1999a). This is an important consideration in assisting people to live longer, healthier lives but with a reduced period during which they may need support. This is termed 'compressed morbidity' and was first introduced by Fries in 1980 (Prophet, 1998a).

There are conflicting views regarding compressed morbidity. Some argue that it is not occurring; others have suggested that it is, but only in respect to some illnesses and disabilities (Grundy, 1998). Its importance should not, however, be in doubt. Prophet (1998b) has commented that compressed morbidity should be "... an explicit policy objective across all departments of government ...", and added that "... it is the greatest challenge for medical science and health education for the twenty first century ...". She also affirmed that "... if morbidity rates can be reduced by 1% per annum, then publicly funded care costs can be reduced by 30%, or £6.3 billion per annum by 2030". Telecare is a potential instrument in achieving this goal.

Older people becoming more consumerist

Much has been made in the US of the 'grey vote'. This refers to the political strength of the older voter, which represents an ever-increasing percentage of the electorate. Older people are in future likely to be more demanding because of their expectations about health and treatment. It has been commented that generally their improved education and economic circumstances suggest they will be less deferential towards medical professionals than the current generation of older people (Wanless, 2001). They are likely to demand a level of service that is acceptable to them and their combined political strength may help to ensure that they achieve their objectives.

The use of technology to support independence

Older people are increasingly encountering a range of technologies. For example, one survey of residents in sheltered housing revealed that 44% had their own video recorders and 45% their own microwave ovens (Brownsell et al, 1999). Familiarity with a technology makes it easier to learn, but this is not solely related to chronological age (RCLTC, 1999). With this in mind the Royal Commission on Long-Term Care expects that in future older people will be as comfortable with computer controls as the present generation are with telephones (1999). The Royal Commission also commented that:

> People constantly look to modern technology to improve their lifestyles. One of the ways in which life could improve for older people is in the harnessing of new technology in new, imaginative and profitable ways. (RCLTC, 1999)

Evidently, the view that older people do not want technology and cannot use it, is becoming dated. Many older people use technology and, as Chapter 5 demonstrates, many welcome technology if a direct benefit can be derived from its use. Indeed, users can actually become the drivers behind the introduction of the new technology. This is evident in an Anchor Trust sheltered housing scheme where, as new technology is introduced, the users are specifying how they want it to work for them.

The power of the Internet

A survey carried out in the UK by Age Concern and Microsoft reported that 4.6 million people aged 50 and over use the Internet (approximately 25% of people over 50), and that 4 million of these have their own computer. Interestingly, 64% of those surveyed commented that having a computer had made a positive difference to their lives, while 81% found computers easy to use. The report also indicated that on average, older people used their computer for 9 hours a week (Age Concern, 2001), and this trend is likely to continue as newly retired people are one of the fastest growing groups of Internet users (Bloomberg Money, 2000).

The Internet could have a significant impact on the health and well-being of people. NHS Direct have a website for advice and assistance and there seems to be an ever growing number of health-related websites. Support groups for specific conditions and diseases are growing and can provide valuable advice and support to people. While there are many benefits of this technology, there are also some pitfalls that need to be addressed. The quality of the information on websites can be questionable, and some sites are couched in professional jargon, personal perceptions, or marketing speak. Efforts are being made to produce a standard, like a kite mark, to indicate that the information is reliable, but at present no such standard is universally accepted.

In a recent Internet discussion, several concerns were raised due to the increased use of data obtained by patients from the Internet (www.futurehealthforum.com). Perhaps one of the key concerns is that patients will require the GP to spend additional time explaining the information the patient obtained. However, in certain circumstances the reverse could be true and the patient could be told where to look to find additional information and support.

In the report based on the debate, Lord Toby Harris, a member of the Greater London Authority, said that:

> The medical profession is going to have to accept that increasingly patients will be arriving with Internet information. This is going to change the balance of power between the doctor and the patient. Instead of being the monopoly provider of information, the doctor will be an information broker and a genuine adviser to the patient. But this will mean a substantial reorienting of the traditional consultation style and it probably has to happen within the next two to five years. (www.futurehealthforum.com)

Mary Granville White, project development officer at Women's Health Information and Support Service, went further and said:

> In the 1960s we worried about patients meeting in self-help groups because of their lack of medical knowledge and certainly there were those who had difficulty – mainly because of the language used by us. Are we again concerned about patients having access to information to question their treatment and make informed choice? Is our concern really all about time? In the long run, won't a better-informed population prove a healthier population? (www.futurehealthforum.com)

A further concern is that medical information from the Internet may be inaccurate and indeed harmful for patients as they may incorrectly diagnose themselves, which may in turn introduce a delay in their receiving the correct medical attention. However, there is almost no evidence that the Internet is harmful to a patient's health. An article published in the *British Medical Journal* concluded that, after an extensive search of major medical databases, only one report provided evidence of a patient dying as a result of their use of the Internet for medical advice. This case involved a patient with lung cancer who died from taking a drug ordered online (Smith, 2001).

Despite this tragic event, the Internet provides real opportunities for education and support if used appropriately. Thus, Australia has embraced both technology and the Internet and a national plan of action has been created that promotes new ways of delivering health services. The plan suggests that the Internet will play an important role in enhancing better care (NHIMAC, 2001). Physicians can also benefit from the educational content of the Internet and in a recent survey of 400 physicians by Boston Consulting Group, 89% indicated that they used the Internet and on average devoted about three hours a week to medical activities online (Health Care Research, Harris Heritage, 2001). Hence, as well as assisting the user or patient in terms of education and support, the Internet also has the potential to be a valuable tool for healthcare professionals.

Conclusions

Unless action is taken to more effectively utilise available resources, human, financial and technical, a healthcare and support system that is already struggling to meet the demands made on it can only deteriorate as society ages and greater numbers of people than ever before require some form of assistance. Technology, and telecare in particular, has been suggested as a possible solution that gives the ability for healthcare to become truly proactive and preventative.

In a review of the ageing population, and setting out recommendations for the future, it is clear that the Department for Trade and Industry envisages telecare and associated assistive technologies as becoming a reality. However, the review makes the point that for "… such schemes to be operating by 2020, planning needs to start now" (DTI, 2000, p 18).

2

Previous trials and developments

Simon Brownsell and David Bradley

'Tele' derives from the Greek word for *far* or *distant* and in its simplest form telecare can therefore be defined as care at a distance, telemedicine as medicine at a distance and so forth. As discussed previously, technology has been suggested as a possible tool in healthcare provision, with one of the most widely used examples being the community alarm system.

Current home-based technologies

Community alarm systems were first introduced in the UK in 1948 on a sheltered housing scheme in Devon where residents activated a bell that sounded in the warden's home (Parry and Thompson, 1993). Technical developments have seen the bell replaced with two-way speech, and when the warden is unavailable a control centre can be contacted to respond to the call. It is thought that some 1.6 million (Randall, 2000) people in the UK have a community alarm, including a large number of people (approximately 500,000) living in sheltered housing. It was suggested in 1996 that there might be 5 million users worldwide (Fisk, 1996), although this figure is likely to be substantially higher now. The basic system structure is shown in Figure 2.1. Once contacted, the control centre operator can reassure callers and facilitate the provision of assistance from anyone with a telephone, the most common contact points being identified in Figure 2.1. However, it is important to recognise that the system cannot respond until the user first makes a call for help, which in some instances they may be unable or unwilling to do.

Figure 2.1: A current community alarm system

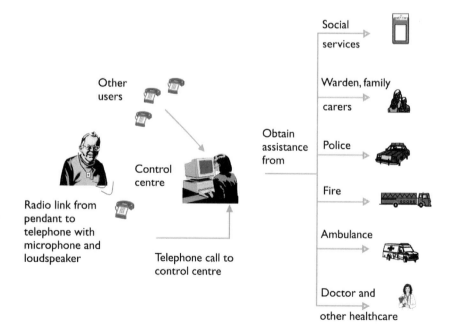

With the exception of the control centre operators, the community alarm system has no integral intelligence and it cannot therefore play a preventive healthcare role. Because no information is provided to the system until the user contacts the control centre, operation is reactive and responsive rather than proactive and preventive. A further limitation of the community alarm system was identified by Thornton and Moutain (1992) who refer to evidence from US studies that some community alarm users perceived themselves as more, rather than less, vulnerable because of the service. However, another US study showed that community alarms save lives, reduce healthcare costs and are well received by users (Hyer and Rudick, 1994). Other articles suggested that community alarms could improve the efficiency, quality and coordination of home-based care (Rudel et al, 1995). A Canadian study of 106 community alarm users indicated that a year after the introduction of the alarm, there was a 25% reduction in hospital admissions and a reduction in hospital in-patient days from 9.2 days to 5.7 (Roush et al, 1995).

Despite the lack of machine-based intelligence in current community alarm systems, an infrastructure is available that could be built on. As identified by Curry and Norris in 1997, "… there was an opportunity to develop rapidly the healthcare delivery side of telecare using the existing community alarm infrastructure. This infrastructure already reaches a group who have above average healthcare needs and often have difficulty accessing healthcare".

Defining home-based care technologies

The use of care technology in the home can be categorised under two headings, telecare and smart homes. Throughout this text telecare is taken to be:

> The remote or enhanced delivery of health and social care services to people in their own home by means of telecommunications and computer-based systems. (Barnes et al, 1998, p 169)

While telemedicine is taken to mean:

> The practise of medical care using interactive audio-visual and data communications; this includes the delivery of medical care, diagnosis, consultation and treatment, as well as health education and the transfer of medical data. (Advisor on Informatics of the WHO, 1997)

Despite their differences, the terms 'telecare' and 'telemedicine' are increasingly being used interchangeably, the difference being that telecare involves the patient's home or non-institutional setting (DoH, 1998a). Nevertheless, both seek to deliver healthcare services remotely using information and communications technologies (ICTs). The qualitative benefits of telecare and telemedicine have been widely published and include:

- the empowerment of patients, obtained through the provision of information, the involvement in the management of their condition, and allowing them to make choices about their treatment (Knipscheer, 1994);
- a reduction in the duration of hospital stays; by implication therefore, a reduction in the costs of hospitalisation, since the patient can be monitored remotely (Curry and Norris, 1997);
- the delay or avoidance of admission to nursing homes (ASAP, 1997);
- improved utilisation of healthcare professionals' time and the improvement of patient medicine compliance (Curry and Norris, 1997);
- accelerated diagnosis and treatment (Wright, 1998a);
- a reduction in the anxiety of patients (ASAP, 1997), and by implication, their families.

'Smart homes', sometimes referred to as 'intelligent housing', or 'domotics' (Berlo, 1999), are all terms used to describe a house or working environment, where devices and systems are controlled automatically (www.smart-homes.nl/engels/). Bill Gates has commented that "… the home itself will almost be like a computer system" (Despeignes, 2000). According to the Consumer Electronics Association, some 7.5 million US households already have some form of 'smart' home. Examples of smart home technologies include door and window openers, heating and environmental controls, lighting, domestic appliances and security devices as well as telephone and video surveillance (Edinvar Housing Association, 2000).

Early smart home concepts assumed that, by the last decade of the 20th century, people would live in 'electronic cottages' supported by an omnipresent artificial intelligence. Although computer and communication technologies have developed enormously over recent decades, these concepts had not become reality by the end of the 20th century. Achieving this goal would require considerable amounts of sensors and data acquisition systems, together with artificial intelligence and knowledge about the local and world environments, ideally incorporating speech input technology and affordable communications. Today, each of these base technologies is available, or becoming so, but the level of system integration is still low (Knipscheer, 1994). Recent predictions continue to suggest that all new homes in western countries will be 'intelligent' from 2010 (Dixon, 1999).

All of the above fall within the global phrase 'assistive technology', which is itself an umbrella term used to describe any device or system that allows a person to accomplish a task they would otherwise be unable to do, or increases the ease and safety with which the task can be performed (RCLTC, 1999). The author of this definition has subsequently acknowledged that it is a very broad concept that could be taken to include items such as swimming goggles or flippers (Turner-Smith, 2000).

Telecare and telemedicine trials

It has been suggested that telemedicine was first practised with the introduction of the telephone (Wright, 1998a). Telemedicine was certainly practised by telegraph in the early 1900s (Anonymous, 1997) and by radio in the 1920s when several countries offered medical advice from hospitals to their fleets of trade ships using Morse code (Wright, 1998a). Among early telecare and telemedicine research was that undertaken by the National Aeronautics and Space Administration (NASA) in the US when they demonstrated that physicians on earth could monitor the well-being of an astronaut in orbit (Wright, 1998a). Additional work in 1957 by Dr Cecil Wittson established the first interactive telemedicine

video link, between Nebraska Psychiatric Institute in Omaha and the Norfolk State Hospital, 112 miles away (Bashshur and Lovett, 1977).

Tele-consultations

A considerable proportion of telecare work to date has centred on the use of video conferencing with, on occasion, additional medical data being acquired. Much of the video conferencing work was pioneered in the US in Kansas where they had available a high bandwidth cable television infrastructure (Lindberg, 1997). When research began, it was felt that a significant proportion of nurse visits did not require hands-on care and that many of the activities involved in a visit could be handled by using an interactive video link, saving the nurse's time spent on travelling. Trials have shown strong nurse and patient satisfaction level with such techniques (Allen et al, 1996). However, contrary to expectations, the trials suggested that technology was not an important issue for the participants, and that the use of technology did not appear to have any negative effects on nurse–patient communication (Whitten et al, 1997).

A 1999 study in the US suggested that 46% of on-site nursing could be replaced by telenursing (where the nurse performs their duties with video conferencing, rather than physically), and that this was likely to be a conservative estimate (Allen et al, 1999). This study also indicated that older people were best suited for telenursing because their problems tend to demand less hands-on intervention. A review of the ability to perform telenursing in the UK indicated that around 15% of nurse visits could be performed remotely, although it was felt that this was likely to bias results towards an underestimation of the potential rather than vice versa (Wootton et al, 1998). The reason for the differences between the US and the UK were due to the greater number of hands-on consultations carried out in the UK.

Investigations into video-conferencing for doctors have also taken place in the US. One trial with 25 patients and a 100-bed nursing home reduced the need for doctors to make home calls and saved many older people the inconvenience and stress of travelling to the surgery. The technology used in the home was based on existing hardware, with additions such as a multi-function patient monitor to which blood pressure cuffs, stethoscopes and other medical devices could be attached. The patient's computer was fitted with a video-conferencing camera which was controlled by the doctor or nurse to ensure the health professional's view (*Electronic Telegraph*, 1997). It could be argued that this does not provide enough information for the doctor, but the majority of a medical consultation is concerned with speech and not necessarily spent observing (Watts and Monk, 1997).

Of course it is possible to perform a considerable proportion of medical interactions by speech alone, as indicated by the introduction of NHS Direct in the UK. This originated from an initiative by the Prime Minister and Health Minister for "… faster and more convenient care" (BBC News, 1998b). Introduced at the beginning of 1998, nurses provide a 24-hour health advice service over the telephone (*CallCentre Europe*, 1998). The aim was to provide people with easier and faster access to information about health, illness and the NHS so that they are better able to care for themselves and their families (DoH, 1997). The service has proved equally popular with both men and women and also with older people (Channel 4, 'No waiting room', 1998). Early in 2000, user satisfaction was tested and respondents who received advice from a nurse found it very or quite helpful in 95% of cases. The most common reason given for finding the advice helpful was that it was reassuring (O'Cathain et al, 2000).

Medical monitoring

Much of the current medical monitoring equipment originates from space or military organisations. NASA has already been mentioned, while the monitoring of military personnel is considered highly desirable. For example, technology indicating which injured solider should be treated first could save time and lives, while increasing the distance between the frontline and medical personnel increases the numbers and safety of people who can assist. For example, in 1995 images of a solider and real-time data such as blood-oxygen levels were sent from Yugoslavia to physicians in the US who were able to prescribe drugs that saved the soldier's life (www.telegraph.co.uk, 9 October 1995). The US military have also developed microchips that can be implanted under the skin to measure and transmit body temperature to a monitoring computer. Similar sensors developed at the Oak Ridge National

Laboratory in Tennessee can be placed inside the ear (*The Times*, 1997).

Over recent years, a number of products for home-based medical monitoring have become commercially available. Companies include, although are not restricted to, American Telecare (www.telemed-care.com), Instromedix (www.instromedix.com), IST/Vivatec (www.vivatec.co.uk), and Shahal (www.shahal.co.il). One of the products of the Israeli Company Shahal is aimed at cardiac patients to prevent cardiac and pulmonary complications in the home. In 1997 they served over 40,000 users and have shown that home medical monitoring improved healthcare control, enabling patients to manage their own health condition with a higher quality of life (Roth et al, 1997). Subsequent analysis by Shahal has indicated that the financial benefits of providing this type of medical monitoring at home is of the order of £575,000 per 10,000 clients a year (Roth et al, 2000).

Medical monitoring is also enabling early hospital discharge. For example, in a pilot study some hospitals in the Yorkshire region are currently discharging people with medical monitoring equipment earlier than may otherwise have occurred. The local NHS Direct site in Wakefield monitors the data and acts accordingly. Patients welcome such monitoring as they can go home as quickly as possible, while also freeing up beds at the hospital.

Life-style monitoring

One of the ground-breaking studies in life-style monitoring was performed by Celler et al in 1995 who indicated that the health status of older people could be determined remotely by monitoring relatively simple parameters that measured the interaction between users and their environment. These parameters provided measures of mobility, utilisation of cooking and washing facilities, sleep patterns and toilet usage (Celler et al, 1995). The study concluded that 50% of the patients had undiagnosed medical problems that could be detected by home monitoring (Curry and Norris, 1997).

This foundation was built on by Anchor Trust and British Telecom, part funded by The Housing Corporation. In 2000, Porteus and Brownsell published the results of what Tang et al (2000)

describe as "… a leading trial in telecare". The monitoring system developed looked for changes in a user's life-style and did not contain explicit medical data. The parameters used to generate an alert were (Porteus and Brownsell, 2000):

- the person was still in bed after the time that movement would normally be detected;
- less activity was detected than usual;
- the use of the refrigerator was noticeably different;
- the room temperature was too low;
- there was a change in the pattern of movements within the dwelling.

To detect these situations, passive infrared sensors were placed in each room of the user's home, along with a temperature sensor in the main living area and magnetic proximity switches on the refrigerator and entry doors as indicated in Figure 2.2. During the two-year trial, more than 5,000 days of life-style data were collected from 22 older people, with the data being collected periodically from the home and analysed remotely by a computer program. Whenever a significant change in behaviour in relation to an accepted *norm* for that person was detected, an automatic alert call was generated. This call was an automatic message that required the carer to respond; if they failed to respond, or could not be contacted, then the next carer on the list would be telephoned, such as the warden/scheme manager, a family member, neighbour or friend. This would continue until a carer acknowledged that they could respond.

The results from the trial were very positive, with 80% of users either very or fairly satisfied with the system developed. The conclusions drawn from the project were that:

- the system is generally acceptable;
- it increases the care choices available;
- it enhances people's feelings of safety and security in the home, reducing their fears and apprehensions;
- it supports and enhances the carer's role.

Smart homes

There has been considerable financial investment in smart homes over the last 10 to 20 years, and several smart home demonstration sites are now in place. Much of the smart home technology can be applied to all user groups, for example, electronic curtain/window closures allow non-disabled individuals control over and ease in their environment. However, for a disabled or older person who may be unable to reach a particular curtain or window, such a device can give considerable independence and security. Nevertheless, some smart home devices are only necessary for particular client groups, for example, a stair lift would not be necessary for all people. Three possible configurations of smart homes are discussed below.

Figure 2.2: A typical installation for a basic life-style monitoring system

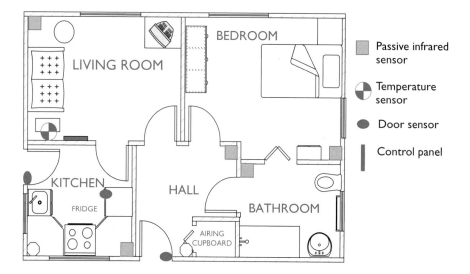

Dementia

It is estimated that approximately 5% of the population aged 65 and over and 20% of the population aged 80 and over suffer from dementia (House of Commons, *Hansard*, col 45W, 30 October 1995). After heart disease, cancer and stroke, it is the most common cause of death in the UK, and the annual cost of providing care for dementia sufferers in England and Wales has been estimated at over £1 billion per year, exceeding the treatment costs of any other single disorder (Research into Ageing, 1997). Consequently, there has been considerable interest in the possibility of technology assisting dementia sufferers with the Dementia Services Development Centre (DSDC) suggesting technology is crucial (www.dementia.com.au/TECHNOLO.HTM).

The BESTA flats in Norway investigated the use of technology in the support of eight people with dementia in a highly staffed environment. The problems that were addressed were the danger of fire, the danger of falling and lying undetected and the danger of wandering and getting lost. Several solutions were implemented (Bjørneby, 1997):

- the lights automatically came on when residents got out of bed at night and automatically turned off when they returned to their bed;
- if during the night a resident was out of bed for more than 30 minutes an alarm was sounded;
- the cooker was automatically turned off if left on by mistake;
- if a fire was detected, then smoke detectors automatically alerted the staff, turned the lights on and unlocked the doors;
- sensors on exit doors alerted staff if they were opened at night.

The results from the trial indicated that staff were *very happy*, suggesting it gave them the security to be able to give better and more confident care. Although an evaluation of the residents was not performed, staff and relatives claimed that the residents felt more confident and safe.

Dementia Voice, in collaboration with Housing 21 and the Bath Institute of Medical Engineering (www.bath.ac.uk/Centres/BIME/projects/smart/smart.htm#bath), have converted a three-bedroom house into a *dementia friendly environment*

(www.dementia-voice.org.uk/Projects_GloucesterProject.htm). The house, referred to as the Gloucester Smart House, was opened in June 2000 to demonstrate technology and allow people to trial the equipment. Installed devices include:

- *bath monitor:* to ensure that the bath does not overflow;
- *locator:* household and personal items such as a purse or glasses are fitted with a small unit that emits a noise when the user activates a control panel. Thus, if the user loses their glasses they can activate the locator and the noise emitted will indicate their location;
- *picture telephone:* shows pictures of friends and relatives, rather than having to remember telephone numbers or the location of stored numbers in the telephone;
- *automatic lights:* when leaving the bed at night the lights are automatically turned on.

Further information on technology and dementia can be found from the DSDC White Paper *The state of the art dementia care* (www.dementia.com.au/techwppr.htm). A useful guide to technology that could be used for people with dementia is the ASTRID guide published by Frisby and Price (www.astridguide.org/final.htm, 2000).

Disabled

Smart home demonstration sites for disabled people include the Rockley Mount Smart Home in Barnsley, which opened in 1997 (see Figure 2.3) (Smit, 1997). This is a joint project between a local school for disabled children and Barnsley District General Hospital NHS Trust (Bassnett, 2001). A standard three-bedroom terraced house has been adapted to include a range of commercially available aids for disabled people, including:

- *door/window openers:* various types of doors and windows can be opened remotely by use of the hand-held device (the Possum Companion – www.possum.co.uk) which controls almost all of the technology in the home;
- *lifting aids:* a variety of different types of electronic lifting aids for users and their family/carers are available for trial;

Figure 2.3: Outside view

Figure 2.4: Technology in the kitchen

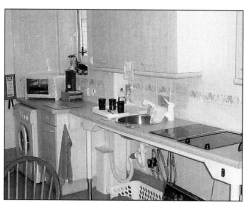

Figure 2.5: Technology in the bathroom

The Rockley Mount Smart Home

- *height adjustable worktops:* allows both wheelchair and non-wheelchair users the ability to work in the kitchen (see Figure 2.4);
- *washing:* several different types of shower are available in the bathroom and bedrooms. The bath can also be automatically filled to the required level and temperature and an automatic electronic dryer is available (see Figure 2.5);
- *stair lifts:* two designs are available demonstrating aids available for both wheelchair and non-wheelchair users.

The house and aids are used by local disabled people to learn life skills. There are plans to widen its use with the introduction of more technology aimed particularly at older people.

General

Perhaps the largest user group for the 'general' category is older people and those members of the general population who use smart home devices to assist them in their daily living. However, it should be appreciated that in certain circumstances such devices may enable an older person to stay living in the community, rather than their having to enter institutional care. There are numerous examples of this approach, including:

- Joseph Rowntree Foundation (1998) and Edinvar Housing Association (2000) demonstration houses in York and Edinburgh, UK;
- Orange 'real live-in research centre' (www.orangeathome/tour_overview.html) in

association with the Universities of Surrey and Portsmouth, UK;

- Millennium Homes (Barnes et al, 2000) supported by Professor Heinz Wolff of Brunel University, UK;
- Trialog (www.trialog.com) of France have validated various devices and the technical feasibility of electronic configurations;
- Matsushita Electric Industrial[1] have the Home Information Infrastructure (HII) demonstration home in Tokyo Japan, that connects "... just about everything inside your home with just about everything in the outside world";
- Philips (www.philips.com/kipsbay/) have created a Smart House in New York to demonstrate their technology;
- West Lothian Council are introducing technology to over 100 homes to provide a better and more cost-effective service for older people (www.tunstallgroup.com/news-WestLothianJuly2000.htm).

As a result of the CUSTODIAN project[2], software is available to aid the process of defining the devices to be included in a smart home for a particular user. The software also indicates the costs involved and provides a useful starting point for users and

---

[1] http://architecture.mit.edu/house_n/web/resources/articles/homeautomation AB%20Jan%2001,%202000%20Technophile%20-%20Home,%20Smart%20Home.htm

[2] (www.rgu.ac.uk/subj/search/research/sustainablehousing/custodian/download/html)

providers. Further information regarding the use of smart homes in social care can be found at www.smartthinking.ukideas.com.

Conclusions

The above review covers the main technologies available for use in support of people in their own homes. However, it is not an exhaustive list. A comprehensive list of current UK-based telecare and telemedicine activity is available at the Telemedicine Information Service (TIS) (www.tis.bl.uk). A similar US version is the Telemedicine Information Exchange (TIE) (http://tie.telemed.org).

From the above it is evident that there has already been considerable financial investment in providing support for people in their own homes. However, it remains to be seen how these technologies fit into the present health, care and support mechanisms currently in place. The next chapter therefore suggests where telecare should be positioned within an emerging policy context.

3

The emerging policy environment

Jeremy Porteus

In recent years, key policies have been established which are driving the technology and seeking to enable older and vulnerable people the support and assistance they need in their own homes. However, housing, health and social care services need to balance out competing demands. Do they promote independence or create new patterns of dependency among older people? Should they be technology or user-led? Are they cost-effective and prevent a move to residential care or hospital admission? Or is it a matter of cost shunting across individual departmental budgets?

The policy environment is rapidly changing and the government needs to address these types of questions, capture the prevalent issues, and ensure that policy can be put into practice objectively and holistically. This chapter seeks to highlight current policies that impact on telecare, while also indicating possible policy developments in the future.

Applying research to policy

The preceding chapters have indicated some of the research and development that has taken place in recent years. Combined with networked communication technologies such as the telephone, Internet, cable and digital TV, many older people can be supported at home in new ways. Life-style monitoring, which was investigated by Anchor Trust, demonstrated how older people can remain living at home for longer – preventing a move to more costly forms of health and social care.

Such findings are crucial to influencing national policy formulation at government departmental level,

in the regions, as well as at a local authority, Primary Care Group/Trust and, in future, Care Trust level, thus, ensuring that the application of telecare meets the expressed housing, health and social care needs of older people irrespective of their housing tenure or accommodation type. The key factor is that a local strategic partnership between commissioners of housing and related support, health and social care, and statutory and independent providers can deliver cost-effective, responsive and high quality support services. For example:

- monitoring of warden call and dispersed alarms in sheltered housing;
- monitoring of building management systems, for example, boilers, power supplies, fire alarms and smoke detectors in blocks of flats;
- emergency access to any building;
- rapid contact with responders, scheme managers/ wardens, family, professional and emergency services;
- performance management issues (time and care monitoring);
- out-of-hours repairs and maintenance services;
- CCTV and security monitoring;
- advice and information services;
- integration with other communication and smart design technologies.

These services were recognised in the Department of Transport, Local Government and the Regions' strategic framework document, *Quality and choice for older people's housing* (DTLR, DoH, 2001), and the Department of Health's recently published 'The National Service Framework for Older People' (DoH, 2001b). Both cite the benefits that technological developments and services offer in meeting emerging housing, intermediate and primary care priorities.

Policy developments and resultant target setting are therefore beginning to see telecare as a means of support, providing assistance tailored to individual needs, and using modern (and older) technology in such a way as to maximise older people's independence and their quality of life. In addition, it can also be cynically seen as a way of measuring providers' performance to ensure that they are meeting national and locally agreed targets.

The modernising agenda: setting the context

The government's modernisation agenda was central to New Labour's first term of office. It sought to dismantle archaic institutional practices, exploit the use of new technology and improve the legislative and regulative framework across housing, health and social care to create 'seamless services'. Within this context, the overriding objective sought to ensure provider choice and better services for citizens. It was and still is seeking to instill a new value base, which:

- empowers individuals, promotes their independence and creates less reliance on the state;
- targets and utilises resources more effectively to those most in need;
- fosters new partnerships between the public, not-for-profit and private sectors in a Best Value framework.

However, with regard to the interface with older people, the report of the Royal Commission on Long-Term Care, *With respect to old age* (1999), noted:

> Making independence a reality requires a change in attitude across society. Improved access to some of the components of a normal life such as housing, education, transport, shopping, social and leisure activities will be essential in an ageing society. Such an approach which represents normalisation, will enhance opportunities for social inclusion and appropriate models of care. (RCLTC, 1999)

It has therefore been crucial that the resultant policy developments have set out how telecare, and assistive technologies in general, can enable older people to live in a home of their choice, receive care and support of their choice, and participate in their community at their choice. A summary of these policy developments is given below.

Modernising social services

The White Paper, *Modernising social services: Promoting independence, improving protection, raising standards* (DoH, 1998b), sought to:

- promote the independence of vulnerable people by improving the consistency of services across the country (for example, National Service Frameworks) and by providing convenient, user-centred services (focusing on a long-term care charter of prevention and rehabilitation);
- improve protection through better regulation of care services through the establishment of the national care standards – there are implications for providers where they provide residential care, domiciliary care (including care in very sheltered or extra care housing) and care services for vulnerable people;
- improve standards in the workforce, including the establishment of the General Social Care Council. There are further implications for providers on performance, staff training and education;
- improve partnerships and coordination across health and social care – the 'Berlin Wall'. This builds on *Partnership in action* (DoH, 1996 at www.doh.gov.uk/pia.htm.) and the creation of pooled budgets, lead commissioning, and integrated provision, and is now further outlined in the 1999 Health Act. Providers need an understanding of these issues, for example, how can services using telecare attract a Promoting Independence Partnership Grant or Prevention Grant?;
- improve delivery and efficiency, including the creation of a Social Services Modernisation Fund (£1.3 billion over three years). Allied to this is the National Priorites Guidance set out in *Modernising health and social services* in 1998.

While there is no specific mention of assistive technology or telecare in the White Paper, there is clear potential for such a dimension. In particular, through the take-up of the Promoting Independence grant. The conditions for each specify the following:

Partnership Grant

- A new grant, providing nearly £650 million over three years, to foster partnerships between health and social services in promoting independence as an objective of adult services.
- Particular emphasis on improving rehabilitation services, avoiding unnecessary admissions to hospital and other institutional settings, improving discharge arrangements, and fostering good joint contingency planning to deal with emergency pressures, for example, Winter Pressures.

Prevention Grant

- A new grant totalling £100 million over three years, for stimulating the development by local authorities of preventive strategies and effective risk assessment, so as to target some low level support for people most at risk of losing their independence.
- Encouraging an approach which helps people to do things by themselves for as long as possible, in their own home.

Modernising local government

The Department for Transport, Local Government and the Regions' White Paper, *Modernising local government: In touch with the people* (DTLR, 1998) sets out the Best Value framework and process for performance management across local authority services, that is, National Best Value Performance Indicators. The priorities for social services are as defined above. Equally there are priorities set out for housing authorities by the Department for Transport, Local Government and the Regions and by The Housing Corporation, the regulating and funding body for Registered Social Landlords (RSLs) such as Anchor Trust. These processes are reinforced under the forthcoming *Supporting People* arrangements.

The link between telecare and Best Value might not be apparent at first. However, it is clear that there will be significant investment in technology and capital to raise the quality of local authority delivered

and commissioned services. This could range from ICTs for management purposes to the installation of telecare in sheltered housing. However, whatever the specification, any investment will require providers to:

- challenge what they do and how they perform;
- compare performances and good practice with others;
- consult with customers and other stakeholders;
- compete and partner with other service providers.

Modernising the NHS

The major policy drivers for NHS modernisation are set out below.

The new NHS: Modern, dependable

This Department of Health White Paper (1997) put together a number of government initiatives to begin to reform the NHS, in particular, moving away from the 'internal market' to an integrated care approach based on partnership. It also set out new requirements for the NHS by:

- developing evidence-based National Service Frameworks (NSFs), linked to improved standards and guidance;
- establishing the National Institute for Clinical Evidence (NICE) to measure the cost-effectiveness of the above;
- creating closer efficiency between NHS trusts and in primary care (provided by GPs and social services);
- requiring health authorities to lead on Health Improvement Plans;
- establishing Primary Care Groups;
- introducing NHS Direct.

Much of this has been outlined in further White Papers and guidance. However, providers need to understand how these reforms impact older and vulnerable people, as well as identifying future investment opportunities such at the greater use of telecare to support the delivery of health and social services.

Saving lives: Our healthier nation

This Department of Health White Paper (1999b) was intended to be an action plan for tackling poor health. It sought to:

- lay the foundation for improving the health of the population as a whole by increasing the length of people's lives and the numbers of years (the compression of morbidity and maintaining well-being/preventive measures respectively);
- improve the health of the worst-off in society, and to reduce health inequalities (four targeted areas for improvement by 2010 – cancer, coronary heart disease and stroke, accidents and mental illness);
- consider the wider social, environmental and economic factors that influence poor health (reflects the work of the Social Exclusion Unit);
- give health authorities greater strategic roles in fostering partnerships with local authorities;
- give Primary Care Groups and now Primary Care Trusts responsibility for public health;
- empower people to make decisions about their own health – access to information, health promotion and choice of services (establishment of the Health Development Agency to replace the Health Education Authority);
- develop/pilot other initiatives, for example, Healthy Living Centres, and extend NHS Direct;
- introduce success measures across national and local performance targets.

Importantly the White Paper expressly recognises the links between poor housing and ill-health.

The NHS Plan 2000

A pivotal strand in the Department of Health's modernisation of health services is the NHS Plan (DoH, 2000a). It outlined:

- the publication of an Older People's National Service Framework (NSF);
- developing care closer to home – the use of intermediate care;
- establishing National Care Standards;
- strengthening partnerships and the creation of Care Trusts;
- introducing fairer funding for long-term care;
- helping older people stay healthy (advanced in the NSF);

- the introduction of Care Direct[1] (advanced in the NSF);
- modernising community equipment services;
- single assessment for health and social care (advanced in the NSF).

There are again close links made to housing and residential services in the NHS Plan and the subsequent NSF. None more so than the reference to Community Equipment Services and the proposed introduction of Care Direct. Both depend on assistive technology and telecare to a large extent and should be extensively referred to in follow-up guidance by the Department of Health.

Part of the NHS Plan is based on a modern and reliable information technology infrastructure. Information for health was published as an information strategy for the period 1998-2005 (NHS Executive, 1998). This was subsequently updated by 'Building the information core: implementing the NHS Plan' in 2001 (DoH, 2001a) and 'Delivering 21st century IT support for the NHS: National Strategic Programme' (DoH, 2002) on 12 June 2002.

Integrating information across various aspects of the health and care systems is a key consideration. The reports also comment that 80% of healthcare episodes are through self-care (NHS Executive, 1998) and that the home is consequently in the frontline. The requirement is therefore for information and services to be made available from the home. The greater use of ICTs will also impact on the way the GP surgery operates, for example:

- ... appointments for consultations or operations can be booked directly – giving patients more choice and convenience, with less wasted time through cancelled appointments and improved management of waiting lists.
- ... more diagnosis is carried out using video and tele-links to hospital based specialists – giving patients more equitable access to care, less waiting and travelling and clinicians more appropriate referrals, improved use of resources and better continuing professional development.

[1] Care Direct seeks to provide information and advice about health, social care, housing, pensions and benefits over the telephone, Internet and at drop-in centres.

• ... test results are ordered and received electronically – giving patients less delay and worry and clinicians less bureaucracy with earlier diagnosis and treatment and improved outcomes. (DoH, 2001a, p 17)

In order to achieve the government's information strategy, a key element is the Electronic Patient Record (EPR). This will provide a single resource for patient information on all interactions with health professionals and save time for nurses and doctors who currently spend 25% of their time gathering or using information (www.shef.ac.uk/uni/projects/ctinm/index.html). The information barriers between health and social services are acknowledged by government who have commented that the "... concern and frustration expressed about the need for mutual access to patient/client records by health and social care professionals needs to be determined and agreed urgently ..." (NHS Executive, 1998, p 31). It is planned that the on-line patient records will be accessible by family doctors, hospitals, NHS Direct, out-of-hours and ambulance services, mental health trusts and social services (DoH, 2000b).

The National Service Framework for Older People

The National Service Framework for Older People (DoH, 2001b) is a key vehicle for ensuring change to health and related services for older people. It applies to a range of services whether an older person is being cared for at home, in residential or nursing home, hospital or intermediate care facility. The eight standards are described in Table 3.1.

There are passing references throughout the NSF to the use of assistive technology and telecare and the

Table 3.1: The National Service Framework Standards

Standard	Description
One	Rooting out age discrimination
Two	Person-centred care
Three	Intermediate care
Four	General hospital care
Five	Strokes
Six	Falls
Seven	Mental health in older people
Eight	The promotion of health and active life

importance of addressing the issue of prevention of ill-health. However, there are no action points or performance measures giving guidance to providers. Nevertheless, it is clear that telecare will need to be harnessed if the NHS is to meet the targets set for each standard. Providers should therefore now be seeking to enter dialogue with health professionals to draw up locally agreed strategies required by the NSF, for example, intermediate care services that promote rehabilitation or unnecessary admissions into hospital.

Modernising support services: Supporting People

The *Supporting People* arrangements are being finalised and will take effect from April 2003. Services for older people will make up the majority of the *Supporting People* programme in terms of the number receiving services, in particular those living in public sector sheltered housing, whether owned and managed by a local authority or RSL.

The programme will introduce a new system of planning, monitoring, and funding for housing-related support services, which will be flexible, cost-effective, reliable and complement existing care services. It gives local authorities responsibility for commissioning and funding support services, previously largely funded by Housing Benefit.

Within the context of Best Value, *Supporting People* will provide an opportunity to develop new and improve or enhance existing services. This includes warden call/community alarm services and floating support services. Indeed, draft guidance prepared by the Department of the Environment, Transport and the Regions states:

Where an alarm service is provided to tenants and is linked to a central calls response team, the costs of the equipment installed in the tenant's home, together with the costs of its installation and maintenance are support costs. (DETR, 2001, p 34)

In the light of the above, local authorities and providers alike should be commencing detailed discussions about how best to deliver these services to older and vulnerable people in their areas, many of whom receive little or no formal/informal support and therefore feel isolated and insecure in their homes.

Modernising housing services

The focus on the modernisation of housing, and improving the housing needs of older people specifically, have been outlined in the following Department for Transport, Local Government and the Regions' (now the Office of the Deputy Prime Minister) documents.

Quality and choice: A decent home for all

Over the last five years there has been significant progress in housing policy terms and laying the foundations for housing in the 21st century. This is recognised in the Green Paper *Quality and choice* (DTLR, 2000).

While not specifically concerned with telecare, it is clear that it can be incorporated in the future. Measures implemented to support older people and people with disabilities include:

* introducing an expanded energy efficiency scheme, providing a wide range of insulation and heating improvements;
* extending Part M of the Building Regulations to make all new housing more accessible;
* introducing *Supporting People* (as described above).

Telecare will inevitably play a major role. This will be by virtue of increased demand for it, because it provides a specific housing solution that meets the needs of older and vulnerable people, for example, providing the platform to integrate the provision of housing, health and social care and support services, while also enabling various smart home elements to support day-to-day living.

To take advantage of this, future policy development will need to identify appropriate means of allocating capital and revenue sources, take into account the extent of the contribution from the private sector, and consider the market drivers, that is, what people are prepared to pay.

Quality and choice for older people's housing: A strategic framework

Published in 2001, the Department for Transport, Local Government and the Regions' strategy paper seeks to address the needs and opportunities for older people in securing decent, affordable and suitable housing and adequate support and care where necessary. Its primary objectives are:

* to ensure older people are able to secure and sustain their independence in a home appropriate to their circumstances;
* to support older people to make active and informed choices about their accommodation by providing access to appropriate housing and services, and by providing advice on suitable services and options.

Importantly, for the first time, there is explicit recognition in the policy arena of the value of new technology in meeting these objectives. The strategy paper states:

> New technology, in the form of telecare and SMART houses, which can be more preventive in their approach, will undoubtedly be of benefit to older people. (DTLR/DoH, 2001)

Moreover, working jointly with the Department of Health, the government proposes to explore these issues further by modernising and integrating community equipment services and promoting the increased use of telecare and environmental control technologies[2] to support the safety and security of older people at risk. It has also set a target of a 50% increase in the number of people benefiting from community equipment by 2004. However, it should be remembered that the government is starting from a low base and that telecare and similar services are still relatively 'embryonic'. There is therefore justification to still tread cautiously through the policy maze.

Nevertheless, providers in the public, not-for-profit and independent sectors are beginning to invest heavily in the next generation of computing, communication and environmental technologies, and are actively developing further prototypes, testing hard and software, conducting market research, and bringing products to the 'market'.

---

[2] This provides an alternative method of controlling battery or electrically operated devices in the environment. For examples see www.rslsteeper.com or www.possum.co.uk.

Yet, it is of fundamental importance that such products can be used easily and enable people to be independent, thereby improving the quality of their lives, that they are affordable, and facilitate further choice and support as and when needed.

Conclusions

As the modernisation policy agenda gains momentum across housing, health and social care, it may be that telecare will inevitably play a role in ensuring that a full range of person-centred services can be effectively delivered. For providers of housing and related health and social care/support services, this is a rapidly changing policy environment and an encouraging one. There is now specific policy, and in a few cases backed by government funding greater opportunities to deliver services which utilise telecare.

This chapter has provided a summary of some of those key policy developments across the spectrum of housing, health and social care. However, providers will also need to take a closer look at the relevant policies and any local priorities to determine how they can make best use of available resources to suit their customer and organisational needs.

With policy supporting developments, innovation and service, it is clear that the momentum behind telecare is growing, but the evidence to support this push is in some respects quite sparse. Questions regarding user views, what form the technology and systems would take, and especially its cost-effectiveness need to be resolved, with the results being fed back to inform policy and local commissioning priorities.

4

Positioning telecare

Simon Brownsell and David Bradley

Healthcare provision can currently be said to operate at three levels, as indicated in Figure 4.1. The *primary care level* is normally the first point of contact and is typically provided by GPs and community health centres. The *secondary care level* provides specialist care in community hospitals, normally for people referred from the primary care level, although emergency admissions can enter directly at this level. *Tertiary* or *super speciality care* is provided by major medical centres for people who require specialist treatment (www.britannica.com/bcom/eb/article/9/ 0,5716,119079+9,00). At this higher level the fewest number of people are treated, as others have been dealt with at previous levels.

In addition to these established levels of care, *The NHS Plan* introduced the concept of intermediate care which provides a "... bridge between hospital and home.... This will speed up discharge from hospital when patients are ready to leave. The new services will give older people more independence rather than being forced to choose a care home" (DoH, 2000a, p 23). This level of care therefore seeks to address a current shortfall where 24-hour care may be provided in hospital one day and the next day no assistance is provided for the person in their own home.

Telecare could be positioned as a form of intermediate care where people could be discharged from hospital and then be provided with a telecare system in their own home. Alternatively, for some people, perhaps with carers or family at home, they could be discharged from hospital and be provided with a telecare system with certain modules of the system then being withdrawn as recovery takes place. In the overall context of health, care and support, telecare can then be located towards the centre of the care structure, as indicated in Figure 4.2.

At the centre of the system of Figure 4.2 is self-care and education, enabling people to support themselves. Although this occurs in the present system, it is not included in Figure 4.1 as the current healthcare

Figure 4.2: The positioning of telecare in the health, care and support system

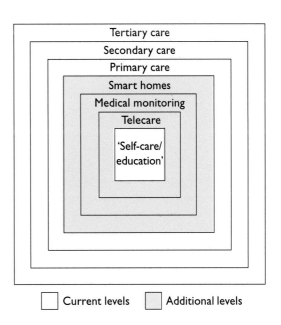

Figure 4.1: The current care pyramid

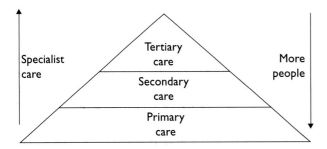

system in the UK has no record of this occurring for a particular individual. With the presence of telecare, self-care can be recorded and provide a bridge between more formal aspects of care. Telecare is positioned outside the self-care level, and may consist of, for example, life-style monitoring which detects changes in behaviour patterns that may require a health or care intervention, while the following level could contain elements of medical monitoring. Assistive technologies, for instance, door openers and stair lifts, may be part of the smart homes level. These first four levels are supported by community care, NHS Direct, and informal support networks (friends and relatives). The accepted levels of care and support can then be positioned around these inner new levels.

It is also recognised that individual levels of care can be accessed directly without going through preceding levels. For example, a user with a telecare and medical monitoring system can go directly to hospital if appropriate. Nevertheless, Figure 4.2 does provide an indication of increasing assistance and need the further away from the centre a particular user is positioned.

In future it may be that telecare, medical monitoring and smart homes are grouped together, as the boundaries between these can become blurred. The distinction between these three levels is in fact an artificial one; as far as the user is concerned they may need a certain level of monitoring and assistance, but which of the levels provides it, is, in many respects, irrelevant to the user.

Potential user groups and services

Table 4.1 indicates some of the possible user groups to whom telecare technologies might be directed, and indicates the wide diversity of provision required, suggesting an equally diverse range of services.

Figure 4.3 and Table 4.2 represent telecare provision as a combination of responsive, supportive and preventative services (Bradley et al, 2002), and depending on the needs of an individual, the relevant services can be provided. Provision in zones A and B requires electronic sensors while zone C is more system intelligence based, using parameters derived from data provided by the sensors of zones A and B.

In practice, many of these devices and systems are reliant on other systems in order to function. For example, in order to accurately generate a fall prediction index, it may be necessary for the user to have a fall detection unit and also to monitor the user's walking and movement.

Conclusions

Telecare has the opportunity to assist a considerable number of people, and in terms of positioning telecare, it may fit between a user isolated in their home and more formal aspects of healthcare provision, such as primary and secondary care. Clearly the opportunity exists to monitor various types of users and to provide assistance when necessary while communicating relevant data to the outside world, that is, health, care and support systems.

Table 4.1: Possible telecare user groups

User group
People supplied with equipment as part of their hospital discharge plans to support early release
People who find themselves temporarily incapacitated
People who require some basic assurances and support in order to lead an independent life-style in their own homes – the 'well elderly'
People with mild forms of dementia requiring some support to lead an independent life-style in their own homes
People undergoing needs assessment, perhaps following a change in personal circumstances
Terminally ill people receiving palliative care at home
People considered as being at risk of accident or relapse
Physically disabled people
People suffering from chronic ailments such as diabetes, hypertension, bronchitis or asthma
People addicted to heroin or other drugs, who are taking part in a controlled course of treatment to enable them to control and manage their addiction

Figure 4.3: Possible telecare provision

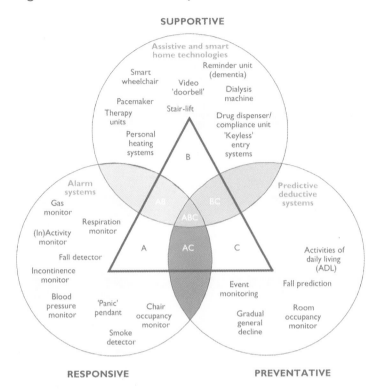

Perhaps one of the key considerations when designing the telecare system is to ensure that the system can adapt and change with the user. To enable devices and systems to be added or removed depending on the status of the user; a modular, plug-and-play system is essential.

Positioning telecare as 'bridging the gap' between the home and formal healthcare provision suggests a re-think in the way services are provided at a national level. If telecare is to flourish and 'bridge this gap' then government policy supporting this is almost a pre-requisite. As evident in the previous chapter this policy is emerging and the next chapter highlights the evidence which can be used to further feed back into future policy developments.

Table 4.2: Possible care provision for the zones identified in Figure 4.3

Zone	Situation	Provision
A	A middle-aged person discharged from hospital following cardiac surgery	Blood pressure monitor Fall detector 'Panic' pendant
B	A person suffering from multiple sclerosis	Smart wheelchair Some automated house functions
C	A person being assessed for living alone following a change in personal circumstances	Activities of daily living (ADL)
AB	Older person living at home	'Panic' pendant Fall detector Video 'doorbell' Drug dispenser/compliance unit
BC	Older person suffering from mild dementia	Reminder unit General long-term monitoring
AC	Older person living alone requiring reassurance	'Panic' pendant Chair occupancy monitor Room occupancy monitor Security system Event analysis system Fall detector
ABC	A person post stroke	Activities of daily living (ADL) Reminder unit Fall detector Chair occupancy monitor Room occupancy monitor Drug dispenser/compliance unit Virtual consultations

Section 2
The evidence

5

User requirements

Simon Brownsell and David Bradley

Community alarm users are likely to be some of the first users of new telecare systems. This is because an infrastructure is already in place that reaches a group who generally have above-average healthcare needs and are familiar with the use of technology to aid their independence.

However, there have been few reports of the views of community alarm users towards such developments. The consultation exercise reported here sought to discover the views of community alarm users in relation to what they would like from their community alarm system in the future. Particular emphasis was placed on the views of people in sheltered housing as, due to their close proximity to one another and above-average support needs, they are likely to be among the first to trial such technology. The study was undertaken in conjunction with a development project being carried out by Birmingham City Council Housing Department to introduce a new, pendant-based, alarm system, while parallel trials were also to take place with some prototype sensors and equipment. The consultation exercise was conducted prior to the implementation of the technology.

In an attempt to establish the real level of interest from users, as many people as possible on the scheme were interviewed. In total 176 users were consulted, representing an 89% response rate which is likely to include those with both positive and negative views. Of those not interviewed, the main reasons were that the warden thought that the interview would cause distress (35%) or that suitable interview times could not be arranged (23%). Interviews typically lasted 30 minutes and covered four main areas:

Control questions: comparison with published figures and investigation of general measures

Present system: examination of the use, knowledge and operation of the community alarm system

Phase 1 alarm technology: requirements of the new community alarm system

Phase 2 alarm possibilities: investigation of telecare elements that could be included in the future.

A standard questionnaire meeting the specific requirements of the survey was not available and a custom-built questionnaire was therefore developed and is provided in the Appendix.

User survey control questions

If the results of the survey are to reflect the population as a whole, control questions are required that indicate how representative the survey sample is to the general population. Various controls were investigated as identified in Table 5.1, indicating that the sample may be regarded as reflective of older people as a whole.

Despite many of the results obtained agreeing with published details, it should be appreciated that those interviewed represent a wide diversity of people, and it would be unfair to group them as dependant people in sheltered housing. For example, 22 people indicated that they would go out of the scheme and into the surrounding area less than once a week, while 11 indicated that they went out more than seven times. Investigation of the number of doctor consultations and the levels of prescription medication also indicated a wide array of people, with 11% not having any contact with their GP during the last year, while 10% had seen their doctor more than 15 times.

Present system

Common home-based technology

It is sometimes suggested that older people do not encounter everyday technology and therefore may have difficulty using advanced community alarm technology. However, Table 5.2 indicates that this assumption is not necessarily correct.

Table 5.1: Comparison of control questions with published figures

Control question	Comment
The percentage of people who live alone	The 1994 GHS (OPCS, 1996) suggests that 24% of men and 49% of women live alone; of those interviewed, 16% of men and 56% of women lived alone
Providers of informal care	Various studies indicate that most carers are female and primarily children; the results of this questionnaire would agree with these findings
The quantity and provision of formal care	The 1994 GHS (OPCS, 1996) witnessed that most formal care was given to women aged 75 and over and people living alone. This finding was observed in the questionnaire results obtained. It has also been suggested that people living alone in local authority accommodation were six times more likely to receive formal care (Government Statistical Service, 1996). The results from this questionnaire suggested a figure of 6.6
Doctor consultations	Analysis of published figures suggested that on average each participant in the questionnaire should have had 6.6 consultations in the previous year, with 1.6 of these being performed in the participant's home. The results from this questionnaire suggested there were on average 6.8 consultations, of which 2.07 were performed in the home
Prescribed medication	One study suggests that on average each older person takes between three and four prescribed drugs on a daily basis (Census and Government Actuary Data, 1992). A further study suggested the figure to be six (Palmore and Burchett, 1997). This questionnaire revealed a figure of 3.7
Hospital admissions	The Department of Health suggests that 32% of older people are admitted to hospital each year (D. Chauman, personal communication, DoH Statistical Division 2 and 3 from Hospital Episode Statistics). The results from this questionnaire indicate a figure of 42%, 10% higher than the Department of Health. However, Birmingham City Council social services suggested a figure of 46.8% for Birmingham, which is similar to the result obtained in this questionnaire
Hospital duration	The GHS suggests for older people an average hospital stay of 12 days (Government Statistical Service, 1996), while the Department of Health suggests a stay of 10.03 days for Birmingham and a stay of 9.5 days as a national figure. This questionnaire revealed a stay of 12.6 days, which is comparable with the GHS results
Falls	It is generally accepted that 33% (Whipple et al, 1990; Richardson, 1993) of older people fall at least once each year. Nevertheless, the results from this questionnaire indicated a lower figure of 24%. For those people who have fallen, published figures suggest that 66% fall again in the next six months (Cummings et al, 1989). Again this indicator was slightly less in this questionnaire, with a figure of 55%
Interaction with family and friends	It has been suggested that 33% of older people are not visited by relatives in their own home during a normal week (Tunstall Telecom, 1997). A figure of 43% was obtained from the results of this questionnaire. In terms of interaction with friends, the same survey suggested that 50% of older people do not have friends visiting them in their own home during a normal week. The results from this questionnaire were slightly higher at 57%

Table 5.2: Community alarm users' experience with common home-based technology

| | Have the technology | | Of those with the technology, the proportion who can use it | | | | | |
| | | | Without help | | With help | | Cannot use | |
	%	n	%	n	%	n	%	n
Cooker	98	172	92	161	2	4	4	7
Microwave	45	78	95	74	1	1	4	3
Washing machine	52	93	95	88	1	1	4	4
Vacuum cleaner	98	173	71	123	4	6	25	44
Telephone	89	157	99	156	1	1	–	–
Television	100	176	100	176	–	–	–	–
Radio	98	173	100	173	–	–	–	–
Video	44	77	84	65	9	7	7	5

A perhaps surprising result was that only 52% had their own washing machine. This is perhaps lower than anticipated as even among households with the lowest tenth of incomes 75% have a washing machine (Down, 2002, p 149). It could be assumed that it would be the oldest people who did not have a washing machine, as these people may not have used one during their lives. However, the average age of people without washing machines was 76, which is the scheme average. It could also be assumed that people without a washing machine were likely to have minimal contact with other technologies, yet of these people, 48% possessed a microwave or video recorder and 19% both. It would appear that the real reason was the availability of the on-site washing machine, which was free to use.

It has been suggested that approximately 80% of older households own a video recorder, but this reduces to a third of single older people (ONS, 1997). The results from this questionnaire suggest figures of 26% and 18% respectively, lower than expected. However, the financial limitations of people living in local authority accommodation may explain the difference. In total, 30% of those interviewed had a video and microwave; consequently the assumption that older people are technophobes and unable to use, or willing to accept, technology is not upheld. Table 5.2 also highlights that those who have technology had few difficulties using them, with the exception of the physical limitations of vacuuming. Furthermore, three (2%) possessed their own computer, with all commenting that they had no difficulties using such equipment.

User satisfaction

The results from the questionnaire suggest that there is universal acceptance and satisfaction with the present community alarm system; indeed, 89% were content with the system. Some 54% indicated that they had used the alarm in the previous year, with the average use being 1.9 times. When the questionnaire was conducted, the only way to raise an alarm was by using a pull cord located in the corner of each room. During the previous year four people had tried to raise an alarm but were unable to reach their pull cord.

Contacting services

Despite many people indicating that they were familiar with common household technologies, and suggesting that they had no difficulties using them, Table 5.3 would suggest that many were unsure of the purpose of the community alarm. This table indicates how users would contact various services,

Table 5.3: Contacting services by community alarm or telephone

| | Community alarm | | Telephone | |
	%	n	%	n
Repairs	74	116	26	41
GP	9	14	91	143
Ambulance	59	92	41	65
Police	52	81	48	76
Fire	44	69	56	88

n=157

only including the responses from people with both a telephone and community alarm, giving a sample size of 157 people in this instance.

Riseborough has suggested that community alarm users have difficulty deciding whether or not a situation is an eligible emergency, and whether to use the alarm or telephone (Riseborough, 1997). The results shown in Table 5.3 agree with her observation as in all of these circumstances the telephone should normally be used. Discussions revealed that many would use the alarm because they thought that this would generate a quicker response. They also believed the police were more likely to attend if contacted by the control centre. However, a significant proportion understand that the telephone would be quicker, but preferred to speak to the warden or control centre operators with whom they were familiar.

Acceptance of pull cords and pendants

Forty-three per cent of homes had at least one pull cord tied up and out of reach, with a worrying 21% having all of their pull cords inaccessible. Figure 5.1 presents these figures and indicates where one pull cord was tied up in which room this occurred.

Occupancy had a significant impact on the accessibility of pull cords. Where occupants cohabited, only 33% had all of their pull cords accessible, compared to 67% for people living alone. A common theme throughout interviews with people living with someone else was that if they lived alone their response would be different. Many of

those interviewed who had all of their pull cords deactivated suggested that if they lived alone they would make sure that all of the pull cords were accessible.

Analysis of the results for each of the three tower blocks highlights the important role of the warden. Of those with deactivated pull cords, 76% were in one tower block, with 16% and 8% in the others. The main reason for the higher figure in one block was that that warden perceived their role as providing information for users to come to their own conclusions, while the wardens in the other blocks believed their role was to ensure that pull cords were available. Both approaches have their strengths, but what is perhaps required is a clear direction to ensure a uniform service delivery.

Phase 1 alarm technology

Alarm architecture

The system in place prior to the completion of the questionnaire was based on pull cords; however, the replacement system would allow users to have a pendant, maintain their pull cords or have both. No financial charge was involved, therefore 60% of those surveyed chose to keep their pull cords and have an additional pendant. Interestingly, 16% preferred to have a pendant and have the pull cords removed. Many of these people suggested that they found the pull cords more intrusive than the pendant, which they felt they could hide under a jumper. Conversely, 24% preferred to stay with their pull cords and

Figure 5.1: The number of pull cords deactivated

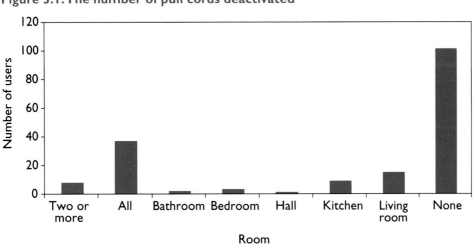

Figure 5.2: Possible positioning of pendants

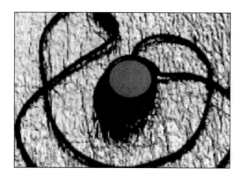  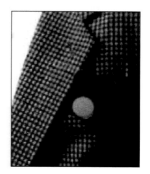

declined a pendant as they felt this option was less intrusive.

The pendant

For those people choosing to have a pendant, three different options were available, as indicated in Figure 5.2. The first of these was the traditional neck cord, the second was worn like a wristwatch, while the final option was a broach that could clip onto jumpers or belts. The choice of pendant was related to gender, with 59% of women requesting the wristwatch, 34% the neck cord and 7% the brooch. A total of 48% of the men had a preference for the brooch, 39% for the wristwatch and 13% for the neck cord. The deciding factor was often concerned with how easily people thought they could hide the pendant.

Phase 2 alarm possibilities

Generated speech

It is common for pendants and pull cords to be activated in error (*Living in Retirement*, 2000) and it was suggested to interviewees that it could be possible for the community alarm to 'speak to them' and inform them the alarm had been activated, providing them with the opportunity to cancel the call. Despite the concerns of some service providers, this proved to be acceptable, with 78% positively seeking such a possibility. For those who rejected this option, the average age was 79, three years more than the scheme average. Overall it can be concluded that generated speech is acceptable to the majority of users if a clear benefit can be derived.

PABX functionality

The Private Branch Exchange (PABX) is a local communications system that allows all of the internal telephones to be connected together with a reduced number of external lines, for example, as found in many offices. Because not everyone is on the telephone at the same time, the PABX does not require as many external lines. The questionnaire concluded that 22% regularly telephone others on the scheme and that on average this would occur three times a week. These people suggested that if the PABX system were introduced, they would call others approximately six times a week. It might be expected that if no charge were involved, people who do not currently telephone others on the scheme may find this beneficial, but only 10% indicated that they would take advantage of this possibility if it were available.

Gas and water

Many (65%) were concerned that others could leave gas appliances on by mistake, with some suggesting that gas appliances should be banned, as a gas explosion in the tower block could impact on everyone. However, many of the interviewees suggested that they had cooked on gas all of their lives, and to prohibit this could be very intrusive.

A more acceptable solution may be to detect the level of gas, and, if above a dangerous level, generate an alarm. This alarm could be internal, perhaps using generated speech, and if the gas level did not decline the gas could be automatically turned off. This would address the safety concerns expressed by interviewees and allow people to continue to use gas appliances. Such technology is already commercially available (Wright, 1998b).

In addition to gas monitoring, a significant proportion of users raised the issue of monitoring water usage. Several commented that they had experienced flooding when occupant(s) above them had accidentally left the bath taps on. Again, devices and systems are being developed to address this issue (Edinvar Housing Association, 2000).

Automatic lights

Automatically turning lights on and providing better illumination when getting out of bed may help to prevent some falls. It may also be beneficial to automatically turn lights on and off when moving between rooms. However, only 24 (14%) were interested in this possibility, but this result may not be representative of users in other sheltered housing schemes or dispersed in the community. A considerable proportion commented that automatic lights were irrelevant because the hallway light for the floor illuminated their passageway. Others commented that they had their own strategies, for example always putting the bedside light on before getting out of bed or using a torch. One lady also suggested that the shock of the lights automatically coming on could give her a heart attack!

Automatic fall detection

The fear of falling and lying on the floor undetected was a concern for many. A system was proposed that would automatically detect a fall, and if that person had not regained their feet within a couple of minutes, an alarm would be raised. In total, 75% commented that they would definitely welcome such a possibility, with a further 2% indicating that they were interested in this development.

Surprisingly, nine people (21%) who reported that they had fallen in the last year rejected this possibility, and it is unclear why this would be so. Two of the nine had fallen six times during the last year and commented that because they fall regularly without harming themselves, such a system would be intrusive. Some also commented that they were uncomfortable knowing that others would be informed that they had fallen, and would therefore rather do without such a device. They believed that if necessary they could raise the alarm with their pull cords or the soon-to-be acquired pendant.

Life-style monitoring

Each interviewee was shown a passive infrared sensor and it was explained that each room would require one. Consequently, if they became unable to get out of a chair or the bath, this would be detected and an alarm generated. It would also ensure that if they normally got out of bed at 0800 hours, but were still in bed at 1100, for example, an alarm would be generated. In the first instance the alarm would be internal with generated speech and then externally to the control centre if the user did not respond.

Many who expressed an interest in this possibility wanted to ensure that they would not experience false alarms and would rather wait for the alarm to be raised than experience a false alarm. Many also wanted reassurance that 'they' – the warden or control centre operators – could not see them.

Of those interviewed, 65% declared that they would welcome such a system in their home, with a further 3% interested in this development. Interestingly, this mirrors the findings of the Anchor/British Telecom work on life-style monitoring discussed earlier. Furthermore, all of the interviewees expressing an interest had no objection to a passive infrared sensor being placed in the bathroom; indeed many saw this as the main source of potential benefit. Table 5.4 indicates that in general the more active interviewees were, the less likely they were to perceive this option as a benefit.

Medical monitoring

Interviewees were shown a photograph of TED, The Electronic Doctor, developed at the University of Wales, Bangor (Doughty and Cameron, 1996), and

Table 5.4: How the number of interactions per week with the surrounding area affects acceptance of life-style monitoring

Outside of scheme		Accept life-style monitoring	
Number	n	%	n
<1	22	55	12
1-5	63	76	48
6-10	85	60	51
>10	6	50	3

Figure 5.3: TED (The Electronic Doctor)

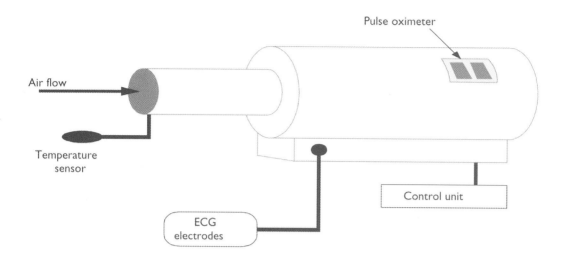

illustrated by Figure 5.3. It was explained that TED would measure blood pressure, heart rate, body temperature and breathing characteristics and that their doctor would define particular parameters for them individually. If the results were outside of these parameters they would be informed and the doctor contacted. The doctor would therefore be able to assist, hopefully before greater intervention would be needed. Cancellation of the automatic call to the doctor would be provided, thereby giving control to the user.

In total, 52% indicated that they would value such equipment, with a further 5% suggesting that they would use it if suggested by their doctor. With such a device it would be assumed that health dictates the response, and indeed this is true both for perceived health and the other health measures. For example, the level of acceptance from those perceiving their health as above average was 43%, while this rose to 54% for those deeming their health as average and 68% for those considering themselves below average.

Video conferencing

To ensure that the user was in control, the system described consisted of a small camera positioned on top of their television that they would physically have to activate to enable video conferencing. Many were interested as to how this would be achieved, as they were concerned about potential damage to their television. In total 44% sought this functionality, with a further 2% possibly interested.

In addition to being able to see people on their television screens, it was also suggested that by activating their camera the person they were conversing with could see them. Of those indicating they welcomed video conferencing, 83% were content with this possibility, while a further 4% were interested.

Effect of age on acceptance

Riseborough's study (1997) of community alarm users suggested that those aged 75 and over were most interested in pendants and 'gadgets'. The results from this questionnaire would agree with her conclusions for age being a qualifier for the acceptance of pendants, but the evidence from this survey would disagree with what was termed as 'gadgets'. Table 5.5 indicates that for three of the enhancements it was those under the age of 75 who were most receptive. However, the results do not overwhelmingly fall into one group or another and

Table 5.5: Interest in the four main technology enhancements, specific to age

| | <75 (*n*=70) | | >=75 (*n*=106) | |
	%	*n*	%	*n*
Automatic fall detection	69	48	80	85
Life-style monitoring	70	49	67	71
Medical monitoring	64	45	52	55
Video conferencing	47	33	45	48

therefore would suggest that the acceptance of the enhancements was not dependent on age. Of the 102 users in this questionnaire with a microwave or video machine, 54% were aged 75 and over.

Acceptance of multiple enhancements

Of those surveyed, 89% were content with their present community alarm system, yet 57% were interested in at least three of the four main technology enhancements and 25% interested in all four. This casts doubt over the validity of user surveys that purely seek to discover the 'success' of current systems as no comparison can be made with an alternative. This questionnaire reveals that despite a high level of satisfaction with the current community alarm system, there is a desire for development.

It may also be considered that previous technology exposure would increase the desire to embrace the enhancements. Of those possessing a microwave and video player, 62% were interested in any three of the enhancements, while this only reduced to 52% of those who did not possess either. Therefore there would be some evidence to support the hypothesis that previous technology exposure increases the acceptance of an enhanced community alarm system, but the results from this questionnaire would suggest the impact is slight.

Video door entry system

The final technical enhancement discussed was a remote door entry system that would allow people to see on their television screen who was at the front door to the tower block. This was the most well-received enhancement, with 92% indicating that they would find this beneficial. It would appear that the high acceptance rate was due to local children causing a nuisance in the tower blocks. To gain access to the tower blocks someone has to let the caller in and this is achieved by activating a switch in any of the flats. Some interviewees commented that some of the "... confused older ones ..." would let anyone in and that being able to see the caller on the television could help to alleviate this problem.

Views of potential future users: the Boots group

A voluntary questionnaire was performed at the 8th Boots Retirement Association Chairpersons' Conference. All retired Boots staff have the option of joining regional associations and the conference gathered together the chairpersons of those regional associations. The 22 people present represent a wide diversity; some were recently retired while others had been retired for some time. They were geographically spread from Edinburgh to Sussex and appeared to have no bias towards accepting or rejecting the technology discussed.

The majority of the Boots participants (21) owned their own homes. Only one was a tenant. Seven people lived alone, eleven lived with one other, while four lived with two other people.

Table 5.6 indicates that members of the Boots group were receptive to the main community alarm enhancements previously highlighted. They were also asked to differentiate between video conferencing with friends and family and virtual consultations with a GP or nurse. Perhaps surprising was that they were more likely to accept video conferencing with medical professionals than with their own family!

Table 5.6: Comparison between present and potential (Boots group) community alarm users (%)

	Current users			Boots group		
	Yes	**Perhaps[a]**	**No**	**Yes**	**Perhaps[a]**	**No**
Automatic fall detection	75	2	23	82	13	5
Life-style monitoring	65	4	31	41	59	0
Medical monitoring	52	5	43	55	40	5
Virtual consultations	44[b]	9[b]	47[b]	36	41	23
Video conferencing				36	23	41

[a] Includes all options except 'Yes' or 'No'.
[b] Virtual consultations and video conferencing were combined in the current user survey.

Table 5.7: How much individual participants (Boots group) would pay for a one-off equipment charge

Amount	£50	£100	£350	£500	£750	£1,000	£1,500	£2,500	£3,000
Frequency	2	1	1	3	1	5	1	1	1

Generally the results from the Boots group and current users are reflective of one another, and give more evidence that such enhancements would be accepted by users.

The members of the Boots group were asked to suggest a one-off figure for equipment and a weekly monitoring charge for a system with the four main enhancements discussed. Four participants did not feel able to suggest a figure as they were unsure what 'technology' costs, but the remaining 16 suggested an average of £925 for the one-off equipment charge. However, Table 5.7 suggests that there is a significant variation between what individual participants would pay for the technology. Table 5.8 indicates the range of weekly charges for the 17 participants suggesting a figure.

When the community alarm is activated, in some circumstances it may be helpful for the community alarm control centre operator to see inside of the home. However, it has been suggested that such a technique is "… recognised as being intrusive" (Ashton, 1997, p 8). The system described would only use the camera when the control centre was contacted and the camera would be hidden, perhaps in the passive infrared sensor used in the life-style monitoring system. The response indicates that all participants would be willing to have at least one camera in their home, with Table 5.9 indicating the acceptance of cameras in specific rooms.

Despite the results suggesting that participants would allow cameras into their homes, the awareness of possible intrusion was evident, especially in areas where people were likely to be in a state of undress, such as the bedroom and bathroom. However, the installation of imaging sensors rather than 'real' images could overcome any concern.

The warden's perspective

Six wardens[1] were interviewed regarding future community alarm possibilities, and were generally receptive to the main enhancements discussed above. All of them believed that the automatic detection of falls and life-style monitoring would be advantageous to users and would also assist them in their job. Medical monitoring was not greeted with such enthusiasm, with just two wardens believing this could help users. One of the other wardens felt that certain people would benefit, while the three remaining wardens felt it could actually be harmful. They thought that providing medical monitoring options to a select few would be divisive, and that some would find it stressful, using it continually to ensure their well-being. There was also concern that users could become dependent on the system, and that medical attention would not be sought because the equipment did not support the user's own feelings that they were unwell.

Being able to speak and see users through the alarm system was seen as advantageous by five of the six wardens, with the remaining warden suggesting that it would be of little benefit. Of the current users, only 44% were interested in this possibility, suggesting the wardens would benefit more than the users. This could be because they may feel that they would be better able to decide whether or not to visit a tenant based on the additional information provided by the video conference.

[1] A warden is a member of staff who manages the sheltered housing scheme and facilitates the on-site care and support. In this survey a warden service was provided during office hours with the community alarm control centre being available at all other times.

Table 5.8: How much individual participants (Boots group) would pay for a weekly monitoring charge

Amount	£1	£2	£5	£10	£20	£25
Frequency	1	3	2	3	4	4

Table 5.9: Acceptance of cameras in the home (Boots group)

	Living room		Hall		Kitchen		Bathroom		Bedroom	
	%	*n*	%	*n*	%	*n*	%	*n*	%	*n*
Accept	59	13	59	13	50	11	41	9	36	8
Reject	41	9	41	9	50	11	59	13	64	14

The control centre's perspective

From a possible number of 18 community alarm control centre staff, 10 participated in a voluntary questionnaire. In a similar fashion to the users and wardens, automatic detection of falls and life-style monitoring were seen as the most beneficial enhancements, with 9 of the 10 control centre staff welcoming these developments. The remaining participant was undecided for life-style monitoring; while a different participant suggested only certain users should have automatic fall detection.

A greater degree of variation was observed for the introduction of medical monitoring. Only two (20%) were positively in favour, compared to 33% of the wardens and 52% of the current users. Six thought certain users should have this capability, one believed that no one should have a medical monitoring device and one was undecided. The use of video conferencing technology indicated that there was uncertainty as to the benefits of being able to see and hear callers. Three were in favour, two thought it would be useful for certain users, two rejected this, two were undecided and one did not answer. A similar position was observed with both the wardens and current users. It may therefore be that both users and providers do not envisage being able to see each other in an emergency as an important consideration.

Validating the survey results

In order to give greater confidence in the results obtained from Birmingham, the questionnaire was repeated at one of Anchor Trust's sheltered housing schemes with the on-site warden performing the interviews. The correlation between results was strong, as can be seen from the summary provided in Table 5.10.

Table 5.10: Comparison of Birmingham and Anchor questionnaire results (%)

Question	Birmingham City Council (n=176)	Anchor (n=27)
At least one GP home visit in the last year	50	60
Do not have any prescription medication	18	10
People who acknowledge they sometimes forget to take medication	16	15
Have relatives who visit weekly	69	66
Satisfaction with alarm system	89	92
One or more pull cords 'tied up' and out of reach	43	30
Replace pull cords with a pendant	24	30
Open front door and answer the telephone with the pendant	92	93
Disguise community alarm as a telephone	64	63
Acknowledged falling in the previous year	24	22
Accept: Automatic fall detection	77	78
Life-style monitoring	68	67
Medical monitoring	57	66
Video conferencing	44	43
Find automatic lights beneficial	13	52

Evidently, the only area where the results significantly disagree is in the potential take-up of lights that automatically turn on and off when required. However, it is quite clear that the overall agreement suggests that the results are reflective of opinions and that present community alarm users would welcome further developments to the system.

Conclusions

This research represents perhaps the largest face-to-face consultation exercise of community alarm users to have been carried out in the UK to date. The evidence is that users would welcome technical advances. Over two thirds of users welcomed the idea of automatic fall detection and life-style monitoring, while in excess of 50% welcomed the possibility of medical monitoring in the home. Video conferencing was the least well-received enhancement discussed, yet over 40% of users would welcome this feature. In time, this figure is likely to grow as people become more familiar with video conferencing.

Supporting evidence from the Boots group of potential future users indicates that they too are receptive to technological development and are prepared to pay a significant amount of money to enable them to stay living independently in the community. Discussions with wardens and control centre operators also indicate that service providers would welcome enhancements to the present community alarm system. This chapter indicates that there is a real user push for developments to take place. Efforts should therefore be focused on maximising the choice available, and to enable older and vulnerable people to continue to live independently and safely in their homes.

6

New generations of telecare equipment

Simon Brownsell and David Bradley

Considering the focus of government policy, the wishes of older people to live independently, and the possible application of technology to support this aim, it is perhaps surprising that little attention has been given to defining the actual 'technology'. This chapter seeks to discover what forms the future technologies should take. A key finding from the previous chapter was that users were prepared to live with a degree of 'risk' and did not want technology to do everything for them or provide a completely safe environment. It is therefore unlikely that there will be one standard system for all, but different system configurations depending on the 'risk' users choose to live with.

It could be argued that for certain users smart homes do too much, as many functions are controlled by the home system. Closing curtains either automatically or via some form of control panel may be beneficial for mobility impaired people, but in other circumstances this may have a negative effect. Thus to some it may be another function that they can no longer perform and may increase any feelings of depression. To others, although difficult, the exercise obtained from such tasks may be enabling them to maintain their range of movements and to live independently. Finding the correct balance so that assistive technologies actually assist and do not bring forward a move 'up the care ladder' is not currently understood, as many of the technologies required are not commercially available. However, when developing the systems and technologies required in the future, appreciation must be given to need and a plug-and-play or modular system is essential to ensure that technologies can be provided when they are needed.

The ultimate aim of a telecare system is to enable people to stay safely in their own homes for longer, while also preventing ill-health. Its objective could be:

> To reduce morbidity through the detection and prevention of the onset of ill health and to autonomously detect when and where emergency situations occur raising an alarm if necessary.

Defining generations of telecare

Perhaps the first step in moving from the current community alarm system, often referred to as a first generation telecare system, to subsequent generations, is to give a clear direction of the technology required. (Doughty et al, 1996) introduced the concept of generations of telecare and in doing so defined them as:

First generation systems: community alarms were considered as the basis of the first generation system. Technically simple, such systems had no imbedded intelligence and are entirely reliant on the user activating a call for help.

Second generation systems: these would have all of the features of the first generation system but would also provide some level of intelligence either locally in the home or dispersed throughout the system. For example, sensors might be positioned both on the user or in the home to detect alert situations and autonomously initiate a call for assistance if required. Second generation systems are therefore proactive and can generate alarm calls if the user is unable to do so.

Third generation systems: these are considered to encompass the detection functions of the second generation systems and to add additional support capabilities such as life-style monitoring. In addition, they would also contribute to an improvement in the quality of the user's life by supporting teleservices such as:

• banking;
• shopping;
• interactive exercise;
• medical diagnosis;
• integration/interaction with other people –
  teleconferencing/video conferencing.

The third generation system focuses on the widespread use of telecommunications and introduces the concept of virtual neighbourhoods (Doughty et al, 1995). Here, irrespective of geographical location, people and organisations can be linked together and the social network of an individual extended to anyone connected to the system. Services can then be delivered directly into the home and greater efforts made to reduce loneliness and isolation.

Tang et al have subsequently added a fourth generation that will involve the use of the Internet to deliver telecare services (2000). However, the use of the Internet to deliver the virtual neighbourhood and teleservices could be considered as implicit in the original third generation system. Despite the work of Doughty et al and Tang et al, a clear description of the components included within these broad definitions is lacking. Based on the views of users and practitioners, technological developments, government direction and the likely speed of organisational change, the remainder of this chapter seeks to indicate the range of possible components in each of these generations of telecare. In so doing, efforts are concentrated on specific telecare developments and not general ongoing developments such as interactive television.

Future generations

Second generation systems (2003-05)

The range of components available in this generation of telecare is defined in Table 6.1.

Table 6.1: Requirements for a second generation system (implementation 2003-05)

Main features	Description	Current status
Fall detection	To detect the presence of an occupant who has fallen and automatically instigate a call for assistance if necessary. It is envisaged that in this generation the user will be required to physically wear a device	Worn devices are available from companies such as Attendo, Tunstall Telecom and Tynetec. However, it would appear that no field trial results have been published and it is unclear how successful such devices actually are
Fire detection	To detect the presence of fire throughout the property and inform the user, if necessary, to contact the control centre	Sensors are commercially available to detect both smoke and heat from a variety of commercial companies
Gas detection	The gas level within the property should be monitored and the user informed as necessary. If above dangerous levels, then the gas supply is terminated	Gas detection equipment is available, for example, Technology in Healthcare and Bongtra, while Attendo and Tunstall have devices which detect the level of gas and can terminate the gas supply
Temperature analysis	Analysis of room temperature and if necessary inform the user of a risk of hypothermia	The use of thermistors is commonplace and they are cheap and effective. Research into the placement may be required to ensure that sunlight does not affect the accuracy of readings

Table 6.1: contd.../

Main features	Description	Current status
Water detection	Suspend the water supply if the bath, shower or sink overflows	A valve inside, or sensor attached, to the plumbing would be achievable and is available by Technology in Healthcare. The detection of water on the floor could be detected by a sensor on the floor, however having activated an alert it may be difficult to reconnect the water supply, as contacts on the floor may still be wet. Condensation on tiled floors in particular may also result in action when it is not necessary
Incontinence monitoring	To indicate when incontinence pads need replacing	The NAIS Care Home in Japan are trialing a sensor to detect incontinence and inform carers when the incontinence pad needs changing (Gann et al, 2000)
Security	Three functions are performed by this component: provide a 'panic button' at the front door and the other functions of a standard burglar alarm; provide a record of when carers arrive and leave the residence; allow authorised access to the user's EPR[a] (Electronic Patient Record) and information services	Intruder switches at entry doors are common on current burglar alarms. Recognition of carers, home helps, nurses and GPs could be achieved through a smart card or thumb print recognition. It is now possible to buy a mouse that will use the user's thumb print to recognise the user and therefore only allow specified users access to a computer (current costs are approximately £100). A further option would include the possibility of iris recognition and if video cameras were already present due to the requirements of other components, this may represent a cost-effective method
Drug dispenser	Dispenses the required drugs when required and reminds the user to take their medication if they forget. Provided in a portable format, so users can take the device away on holiday, for instance. The dispenser should connect to the Intelligent Home Alarm System (IHAS) and allow interrogation remotely by medical professionals	Manual medication dispensers are available for a week at a time. Basic tablet dispensers are also available from Attendo and IST, although they do not provide the functionality discussed
Life-style monitoring	To detect changes in the life-style of the occupants(s) that may indicate that assistance is required. The system should include the ability to learn and adapt to the user, probably through some form of neural network. This would minimise the potential for false alerts	The potential of life-style monitoring has been highlighted in the Anchor Trust/BT trial (Porteus and Brownsell, 2000). However, this trial did not provide the processing necessary to alter the maximum times in given rooms. It was also not possible to detect with a degree of certainty, situations where two or more individuals lived together. In order to achieve this with the use of passive infrared sensors used in the Anchor Trust/British Telecom trial it may be necessary for users to wear an electronic tag to differentiate from one another. A tag would also be required with moving pets, such as a cat or dog, differentiate between the movements of the user and a pet

Table 6.1: contd.../

Main features	Description	Current status
Medical monitoring	To measure the medical characteristics of users and facilitate a call for assistance if outside of allowable parameters. It is envisaged that the equipment will be a stand-alone device used when necessary rather than worn on the body. This is due to the perceived intrusion of such monitoring and the likely performance of worn devices	Equipment supplied for example by Instromedix and American TeleCare provide ECG (electrocardiogram) and other readings. However, the integration of this equipment with the other modules is not currently available. Thermography (infrared) could also be a possibility but is not currently available. In addition to using standalone medical equipment, information for diabetes and other illnesses indicated by a change in urinary sugar levels could be gathered from an 'intelligent toilet'. Such a system is currently being developed in Japan (Burley et al, 2000)
Virtual consultations	Enable medical consultations to take place following an alert from the medical monitoring component or replace a standard home/surgery-based GP visit. Also enables video conferencing with friends and neighbours on standard telephone	Virtual neighbourhoods on a one-to-one basis exist but are relatively 'slow' when using ISDN2 (Integrated Services Digital Network, 128kb/s) and may be regarded as impractical lines. ISDN6 (384kb/s), ADSL (Asymmetric Digital Subscriber Line, which adapts the existing telephone line to provide fast data transfer of up to 2Mb/s) and other advanced networks are available and provide the necessary transmission speeds, but may be considered as cost prohibitive currently. Cameras are available and are appropriately small with suitable resolutions. Standalone video conferencing equipment is available from a number of suppliers such as MotionMedia and Vspan
Intelligent Home Alarm System (IHAS)	This is the hub of the home-based equipment and provides control to the various components of the home-based technology; communicating with the user(s) and external organisations	Communication between modules is attainable with present technology, for example Bluetooth. Communication for people with hearing problems is also attainable with current technology
Electronic Record Patient (EPR)	Contains all of the information regarding a particular user, also controls access to ensure that only information relevant to a particular user (GP, control centre operator, home help etc) is available to them	In theory such databases are available but none exist which specifically cater for the needs as set out above. The government has indicated that by 2005 all acute trusts should have access to level 3 EPRs[b]
GP surgery	Provide medical assistance and video consultations	The basic technology needed is available
Control centre	Provide support to users and facilitate appropriate response to user/system generated alerts. Also take ownership for the data held within the whole system	Call handling systems are available but need to be amended to provide the facilities above and integrate in the manner suggested
Hospital health services	Facilitate medical assistance and suspend and reinstate home care as necessary (information provided by updating the EPR)	The government had indicated that by the end of 2002 GPs will be able to access the hospital's records through the NHSNet (DoH, 1997). Access to a users care package is possible but not currently performed

[a] Further information on EPRs can be found at www.doh.gov.uk/ipu/whatnew/eprdefv3.htm.
[b] Refer to www.doh.gov.uk/nhsexipu/strategy/overview/sect02.htm.

Table 6.2: Possible modular second generation telecare system

Level	Description	Modules
One	Current community alarm system with speech synthesis for false alarms and a security system	Fire detection Security IHAS EPR Control centre GP surgery Hospital health services
Two	In addition to the above system, automatic fall detection and life-style monitoring	Fall detection Life-style monitoring Temperature analysis
Three	In addition to level two, medical monitoring and video conferencing	Medical monitoring Virtual consultations and neighbourhood

It is unlikely that any user would have all of the components, but rather a range is available from which those most appropriate to a particular user can be chosen or be prescribed, for example, to meet a specific health condition or social services requirement. As needs change over time, new components can be introduced, while in the example of early discharge from hospital it may be appropriate to withdraw certain components as the user becomes more independent. To aid in the assessment process it is envisaged that three standard second generation systems be generally available, as indicated in Table 6.2. In addition, Table 6.3 suggests further modules that can be added at any of the levels identified in Table 6.2.

Overall, the second generation telecare system provides greater support and monitoring and removes the constraint of the user having to initiate a call for assistance. Automatic call generation and monitoring is provided through a number of new or emerging technologies, such as drug dispensers, automatic fall detection, or life-style monitoring. Each of the technologies included in the second generation system can be provided on an individual basis so that

a user may have a fall detection unit without a drug dispenser or life-style monitoring. The system is therefore truly plug-and-play, or modular, and able to address the particular 'risks' of individual users. The intended users are the present community alarm users, while modules of the system may also benefit people in residential care or nursing homes.

User information is currently distributed across many service providers. In the second generation system this information is grouped together into an EPR (Electronic Patient Record). The information from health, housing and social services is maintained in one place; however, access to the information is on a need-to-know basis. Therefore, if a carer accesses the EPR, only information relevant to them will be available, whereas a doctor would have access to medical information from the hospital and general practice. Due to the additional monitoring in the user's home, the information gathered by the life-style monitoring modules and so on is stored for future analysis and is also actively used to alert healthcare and other professionals of situations that need further investigation.

Table 6.3: Examples of additional modules based on specific need

Module	Possible reason for installation
Gas detection	Signs of forgetfulness
Water detection	Signs of forgetfulness
Incontinence monitoring	Any user with incontinence
Drug dispenser	History or possibility of poor compliance to drug regime

Assistance with medication can also be provided, including prompting users to take their medication if they forget. Early detection of general medical problems can be recognised through medical monitoring equipment and, following agreed protocols, any identified problems routed to a medical professional for advice and/or examination if appropriate.

The home also becomes a safer environment in terms of the appliances used and the detection of emergency situations, such as a fall, fire or the presence of intruders. The system automatically calls for assistance when pre-defined conditions arise, and access to the Internet or virtual neighbourhoods should be available for people with health or mobility problems if it is thought that such access could be beneficial.

Third generation systems (2005-10)

Built on the anticipated success of a second generation system capable of detecting some emergency situations and medical parameters, the third generation system introduces additional monitoring capabilities. The performance is also enhanced to enable conditions requiring attention to be detected earlier. Improvements in medical monitoring will enable further parameters to be measured, while for some users continuous 24-hour medical monitoring will be possible. The introduction of expert systems (software applications that function as if an expert human consultant) enables further analysis to enable prevention to play an increasing role.

Any GP surgeries that had not previously obtained access to the EPR or video conferencing should now obtain access and become a component of the overall system.

Overall, the third generation system is enhanced and made more flexible and responsive. Tasks that were previously carried out by staff but did not require contact with users are taken over by the system. This therefore enables staff to spend more time with users and to provide a more caring environment. The range of components available in this generation of telecare is defined in Table 6.4.

Fourth generation systems (2010-20)

The focus of the previous generations was to monitor users and detect emergency situations. Attention was also given to prevention in respect to medical parameters, while the introduction of expert systems enabled the system to ensure that medication was prescribed correctly. The fourth generation system builds on these previous generations by developing the system for both the user and provider.

For the user, intrusion is reduced with implanted sensors under the skin so that the user no longer has to wear a pendant or similar device when in the home. When outside of this environment, the implanted sensors work in the same way as the medical band module, communicating with the distance support module. Assistance with tasks of daily living enable users to stay independent in their own homes for longer, automatic robots conducting tasks such as cleaning.

Medical professionals received support from expert systems in the third generation system and developments in artificial intelligence will further enable remote assessment. The Activities of Daily Living (ADL) has conventionally been used by social services in assessing older people's need for long-term care (RCLTC, 1999); however, this often annual 'snapshot in time' assessment has often failed to assess the user as their needs change, which is especially relevant after hospital discharge. The fourth generation system addresses this deficiency by monitoring the user on a daily basis and automating the assessment. Users can then be formally assessed after the system has indicated that intervention would be beneficial. This allows resources to be effectively targeted and truly allows for a preventative system, both in terms of the user's health and their daily living.

Any pharmacist that had not previously obtained access to the pharmacy database should now obtain access and become a component of the overall system. The main features of the fourth generation system are described in Table 6.5.

Table 6.4: Requirements for a third generation system (implementation 2005-10)

Main features	Description	Current status
Components of second generation system	The previous modules are available in the third generation system	As described above
Life-style monitoring	Identify the movements of multiple users without having to use tagging; also measure the user's gait and how often they climb stairs (if present). The amount of time actually sleeping should be recorded; while a list should be maintained of favourite television programmes to minimise the number of false alarms if a favourite programme changes its time	Acoustic signature (sound) and video cameras could both be possibilities; however, developments would be necessary to meet all of the requirements. Gait analysis has been achieved by wearing a device above the knee (Miyazaki, 1997), but acceptance would be questionable. Force plates on the floor and camera systems (Whipple et al, 1990) can be used but cost could be inhibiting on a large scale
Security	More developed burglar alarm and automatic recognition of the user	The second generation security module explained that the equipment needed to meet these requirements exists. Nevertheless, the individual elements would need to be brought together
Weight detection	Measures the user's weight	Weight detection through pressure sensors or force plates is available and could be used to meet the requirements of this module. Another possibility would be to measure weight when the user is sitting on the toilet seat and is currently being investigated in Japan[a]
Drug dispenser	Enable repeat prescription reminders and remote analysis of the medication held within the dispenser	It would appear that no device currently exists that meets these requirements; however, with the present state of technology, an effective device could be produced
Medical band	Provide 24-hour continuous medical monitoring for users wearing a medical bracelet or vest. When outside of the home the medical band should only raise an alarm if immediate medical attention may be required, communicating through the distance support module	An American device by VivoMetrics is capable of measuring 40 physiological signs of sickness and health. A medical band is available from Vivatec that measures the general physical activity of the wearer together with pulse rate and temperature. Communication between the medical band/vest and the distance support module could be achieved through Bluetooth etc
Distance support	Communicate with the medical band and allow the user to call for assistance when away from home	SAFE 21, Social Alarms For Europe in the 21st century[b], Barnsley District General Hospital and the Universities of Northumbria, Dundee and Bristol are developing a mobile phone that will contact a control centre when an emergency button is pressed, using Global Positioning System (GPS) to provide the position of the caller. Communicating with the medical band is not foreseen as a problem but the physical size of the equipment may be

Table 6.4: contd.../

Main features	Description	Current status
Intelligent Home Alarm System (IHAS)	The ability to track the user if they fail to return home at a specified time. For example, the user may say "I'm going to Mrs X, I'll be back at 10". The IHAS should ensure that the details of Mrs X are known and that the 10 refers to am or pm. If the user fails to return a pre-defined time after that specified, then Mrs X can be contacted through the IHAS and action taken depending on the reply (if present)	Discrete or single word speech recognition through the telephone system has proved successful in trials, although continuous, natural speech is currently not possible through the telephone system (Attwater and Whittaker, 1996). For large vocabularies the accuracy of automatic speech recognition is unlikely to be above 87% at present[c]. As such, this may not be sufficient for speech communication with the IHAS. The accuracy for users with speech disorders is likely to reduce accuracy further as speech is often weak, slow or imprecise. However, work is currently ongoing at Barnsley District General Hospital and the University of Sheffield to produce speech recognition equipment for people with severe dysarthria[d]. The use of speech synthesis with telephone messages is available and has proved to be successful (Porteus and Brownsell, 2000)
User control	Provide verbal communication with the home-based system	Requires automatic speech recognition and was discussed under the IHAS module
Virtual GP/ neighbourhood	Provide remote physiotherapy and exercise schemes	Technically it is possible to achieve the requirements of this module if there is a suitably fast transmission speed into the user's home. 384 kbit/s would seem suitable for good quality video conferencing. A remote physiotherapy project has recently commenced with the University of Abertay Dundee, Sheffield University, Sheffield Hallam University and Barnsley District General Hospital
GP surgery	Expert system to suggest to the GP what medication they could prescribe	An expert system for monitoring psychiatric treatment has been created. It identifies deviations from established practice standards (covering the evaluation, diagnosis and treatment of psychiatric disorders) and issues information alerts about these events (Bronzino et al, 1995). It does not appear that an expert system that is up-to-date for general practice has been created, although decision support systems for antibiotics are becoming available[e]
Pharmacist	Enable paperless prescription and facilitate delivery of prescriptions to mobility impaired users	No such system currently exists; technically the functions could be delivered but communication between the relevant agencies is likely to be a stumbling block. Nevertheless, the government have suggested that electronic prescribing between medical centres will be available by 2004[f]

Table 6.4: contd.../

Main features	Description	Current status
EPR	Store the user's data	Enhancements to the database would be trivial if the database was originally set up to anticipate additional fields and viewpoints
Control centre	Support for foreign languages and analysis of users EPRs to ensure that correct medication is being used	Call handling is available but the expert systems are not. Birmingham City Council has experimented with a language translation system but has not completed the project (personal communication with Careline manager, Birmingham City Council, Housing Department). It is unlikely that successful systems will be available until voice recognition becomes more accurate
Hospital health services	No change when compared to the role undertaken in the second generation system	Available

[a] Refer to www.devicelink.com/mddi/archive/00/01/012.html.
[b] Refer to www.tunstallgroup.com/news.
[c] Refer to www.abilitynet.co.uk.
[d] Refer to www.dcs.shef.ac.uk/~pdg/stardust.
[e] Refer to www.federaltelemedicine.com/n043001.htm.
[f] Refer to www.doh.gov.uk/pdfs/pharmacyfuture.pdf.

Table 6.5: Requirements for a fourth generation system (implementation 2010-20)

Main features	Description	Current status
Components of second and third generation system	The previous modules are available in the fourth generation system	As described above
Water detection	Monitor the washing habits of the user	A valve inside, or sensor attached, to the plumbing would be achievable or acoustic signature may be a possibility, as long as it could be distinguished whether the bath, shower or sink was being used
Incontinence detection[a]	Detect the onset of incontinence	A technology to meet this specific need does not appear to have been developed. However, research has enabled computer systems to smell[b] and this may be a possibility
Robotic assistance	Provide mechanical assistance with vacuum cleaning, retrieving items from the floor and dressing	Commercial robotic vacuum cleaners are becoming apparent at a cost of around $1,000 (approximately, £600); however, currently they are only able to operate on flat surfaces[c]. Robots to reach, pick up and manipulate objects are also being developed (Hagan et al, 1997)
Virtual GP and neighbourhood	The scanning of letters and forms that cause distress. Assistance being provided from friends or relatives, and ultimately the control centre or social services if necessary	Scanning equipment is already commercially available although consideration to usability may be required to ensure that users can operate the equipment successfully
Implanted medical monitoring	Implanted sensors measuring vital signs 24-hours a day	Several million 'injectable computers' consisting of a chip, power generator, transmitter and receiver were created in 1998 by companies such as Datamars in Switzerland[d]. It has been suggested that implanted sensors will be in widespread use by 2010 (Dixon, 1999)
IHAS	Route emergency fire calls directly to the fire brigade	As defined in the third generation system
User control	The use of the mind to control electronic devices around the home	Controlling a switch by the mind is already possible and it has been suggested that such systems will be common place by 2010 (Boothroyd, 1997)
Control centre	Through an expert system, each user's EPR is analysed under the automatic ADL assessment	The call handling could be performed with current technology; however, it would appear that the expert system does not exist in a suitable format

[a] Older women who experience incontinence are two times more likely to enter nursing care, and for men the likelihood is trebled. Incontinence affects 5% of the adult population in the UK and it is estimated that associated health costs are £1.4 billion per annum (Research into Ageing, 1998).

[b] Refer to www.digiscents.com.

[c] Refer to www.eureka.com/whatsnew/robotvac.htm.

[d] Refer to www.globalchange.com/skinchip.htm.

Conclusions

The present community alarm or first generation telecare system serves approximately 1.6 million people in the UK and is acknowledged as being technically simplistic. It is constrained by the user having to initiate a call for assistance which they may be unable or unwilling to do. Enhancements have been discussed throughout recent years but little attention has been given to defining the technology that should be available.

Based on the views of users and technology developments, this chapter has indicated possible components for new generations of equipment. However, while it may be acknowledged that such systems may be beneficial to users, the associated costs and service implications must be understood if they are to be introduced efficiently and effectively. The next two chapters investigate the implications.

7

The cost benefits of telecare

Simon Brownsell and David Bradley

The development of new generations of telecare equipment has a tremendous potential to assist users to live independently and safely in their own homes. However, for telecare to become accepted practice, it is necessary to understand how its introduction might impact on costs and human resources.

Despite the requirements for a cost analysis of telecare, little has been published, and it has been said that this has mitigated against the further development of such services (Fisk, 1998). In an effort to address this deficiency, a cost analysis model has been created (using Microsoft Excel) and reported elsewhere (Brownsell et al, 2001). The model has been used to compare the present community alarm system in Birmingham City Council with the hypothetical second generation telecare system defined in the previous chapter.

Model assumptions

The approach adopted for the cost analysis model is that of a quantitative analysis based on quantifiable and attributable costs, where only those costs required for the purposes of decision making have been included, as described by Drury (1994). Throughout the analysis, assessment of the potential of equipment and possible costs has been based on available information. Where possible, government or other authoritative published figures have been used. Thus, when calculating the number of people aged 65 and over admitted to hospital per annum, a figure of 32.4% has been used. This is derived from information provided by the UK Department of Health (personal communication, DoH, Statistical

Division 2 and 3 from Hospital Episode Statistics, June 1998), and has greater authority, even though for the city of Birmingham, which is used as an example of current practice in the model, a figure of 46.8% may be more appropriate (personal communication, Birmingham City Council, social services, June 1998).

Where government or published figures are not available, input from professionals has been used. Where conclusive agreement between professionals is not available, any possible savings have been disregarded. Hence, while it is generally agreed that early detection of fires will result in a saving for the fire service as well as in reduced building damage, quantifying this prospective saving has proved difficult and it is not therefore included in the analysis.

Throughout the development of the model, assumptions have been made regarding the benefits and costs involved. A summary of applied assumptions is given below.

- The transmission speed of the present telephone system is not generally sufficient for video conferencing; in reality ISDN, some form of DSL (Digital Subscriber Line) or a communications system using mains cables may be required. The necessary cost for such systems has not been included due to the uncertainty of possible charges. The history of telecommunications suggests that these costs are likely to fall with time. Comparison is therefore made with an average running cost, namely a 4.2p minimum charge for short calls and an average of 1.5p a minute for calls in excess of the imposed minimum charge.

- Throughout the analysis it is assumed that each user has a telephone (93% of older households had a telephone in 1994 [OPCS, 1996]).
- For the purpose of costing, all present and proposed users have a pendant system.
- For the present system the life expectancy of home-based equipment is five years (personal communication, Careline manager, Birmingham City Council, Housing Department), while for the proposed system this is expected to increase to 10 years. Life expectancy of warden scheme and control centre equipment is identical.
- The model assumes that Birmingham has 11,618 community alarm users, living in sheltered housing and/or the general community.
- 5% of units and 18% of pendants need replacing annually with the present system (personal communication, Careline manager, Birmingham City Council, Housing Department); it is estimated that this will reduce to 3.5% of units and 16% of pendants with the proposed system. A 'faulty' home unit in the present system is replaced with a new unit, while the proposed system with self-testing will indicate which module needs replacing at a cost of £30 per hardware module, not including fitting. The cost of a replacement pendant is £50, plus fitting for both systems (personal communication, Careline manager, Birmingham City Council, Housing Department).
- The proposed system requires a small sensor unit in each room; in certain rooms and dwellings mains power will not be available; it is thought that this may account for 90% of users each requiring an average of five batteries. The remaining 10% have fully hard-wired systems with mains power. Battery life is expected to have a mean of five years and require replacement by a trained installer, not a warden, friend or family member.
- Hospitals have access to the pool of data held at the community alarm control centre without incurring additional costs. It is presumed that the data collection costs on admittance with the present system will be the same with the proposed system. However, a saving in time is highly probable with the proposed system and therefore a further potential saving.
- Human resources are available and transferable; therefore additional community carers are available where necessary.

- No borrowing is needed in year 1 for the present system. Only expenditure in addition to this is subjected to borrowing at the base rate of 6%.
- No borrowing is required in year 5 for the present system to replace existing equipment.
- The residual value of assets (the value of an asset at the end of its 'useful economic life') is said to be zero.
- Where specific figures for community alarm users are not evident, it is assumed that figures for older people can be used. This is based on 87% of the community alarm users in sheltered housing in Birmingham aged 65 and over (personal communication, Careline manager, Birmingham City Council, Housing Department), while the average age of new tenants entering Anchor's sheltered housing schemes is around 82.

System costs

As with all new and complex technologies the cost of a new generation of equipment is likely to be substantially higher than the present, more basic first generation system. One of the merits of the second generation system is that users would have system and technology modules tailored to their specific need or identified level of 'risk'. Therefore, some users would have several of the modules described in the previous chapter, while others may have a more basic system. In addition, many of the technology modules do not exist or are prototypes, while the costs of technologies change rapidly over time. These variables therefore make it difficult to estimate the likely system cost. However, Table 7.1 indicates the anticipated initial expenditure at varying average costs for the home-based technology.

Table 7.1 provides estimates of the initial expenditure assuming the proposed average costs for second generation home-based equipment were £500, £700, and £1,000 respectively. As previously discussed, only those costs required for the purposes of decision making are included. Therefore, the figure of £141,000, equivalent to £1,000 per warden scheme in Birmingham, indicates the additional computing costs required for the proposed system, in addition to the warden scheme costs in the community alarm system. Similarly, for the control centre, both systems require a control centre but it is expected that the additional requirement for the management of each

Table 7.1: Prospective system costs for different average installation costs

Technology costs	Present system	Cost (£) Advanced telecare system		
Technology cost of home-based equipment	£175	£500	£700	£1,000
Home-based equipment cost	1,909,000	5,362,000	7,487,000	10,675,000
Warden schemes		141,000	141,000	141,000
Control centre		50,000	50,000	50,000
GP and nurse equipment		241,000	337,000	482,000
Installation and training	279,000	531,000	550,000	579,000
Total initial expenditure	4,097,000	6,325,000	8,565,000	11,927,000

user's EPR will involve an additional infrastructure expenditure of £50,000.

The proposed system also makes use of video conferencing and virtual consultations; the cost of this equipment is anticipated at 80% of the home-based equipment cost. The model assumes that all 574 GPs in Birmingham have their own equipment along with 19 nurses. In financial terms, when deciding whether to use the community alarm or proposed second generation telecare system, it is evident that the proposed system would require considerable initial expenditure over and above the cost of the present community alarm system.

Maintenance costs

Currently, if a fault occurs in the home-based equipment, then it is normal practice to replace the unit at a cost of £175. Due to more advanced fault reporting in the proposed system, the faulty unit is assumed to be repaired at an anticipated cost of £30 plus fitting. However, the proposed system has additional technology in GP surgeries that will also require maintenance. Overall, the present system costs £227,000 per annum, while the proposed system costs £161,000, saving approximately £60,000 per annum or £0.6m over a 10-year cycle. Evidently, if the additional expenditure on the proposed system is to be justified (on financial grounds), then considerable operating savings will need to be made.

Running costs

The proposed telecare system is technically more advanced and its introduction will have the opportunity to identify situations earlier and prevent hospital admissions. When compared to the present system the changes anticipated are described in Table 7.2.

Using these service delivery changes within the cost analysis model reveals that there is the potential for significant savings, as identified in Table 7.3. It should be noted that the calculations are based on a participating population of 11,618, and not the total number of older people in Birmingham.

Figures suggest that the NHS costs around £115 million a day to run (Murray, 1998). Table 7.3 indicates that the adoption of the proposed system in a city such as Birmingham could save in the region of £475,000 in operating costs during the first year of operation, increasing to £1,500,000 in the fifth and subsequent years. It should be noted that such sums only take into account relevant costs such as 'bed blocking' and occupancy rates, and not the totality of possible savings across the local housing, health and social care economy. It is believed that further savings could be evident if more specialised equipment was provided for general patients on a short-term basis after discharge. However, work is required to identify those people who would benefit most.

Table 7.3 also indicates that one of the most significant savings is in the area of residential care. This is due to a reduction in the number of people in care declared in Table 7.2, and the 'delay' in entering care – the duration of the delay is taken at eight weeks in the model. Further reductions after year 4 are not evident because the variables defined in Table 7.2 do not alter from this point.

Table 7.2: Service implications for the proposed telecare system

Effect on service providers of proposed system – community alarm users only	Present system	Operational year of the proposed telecare system										
		1	2	3	4	5	6	7	8	9	10	
Reduction in GP surgery consultations (physical and virtual)		0	0	0	0	0	0	0	0	0	0	%
Reduction in GP home visit consultations (physical and virtual)		0	0	0	0	0	0	0	0	0	0	%
Percentage of GP surgery consultations to become virtual		10	12.5	15	17.5	20	22.5	25	27.5	30	32.5	%
Percentage of GP home visit consultations to become virtual		15	17.5	20	22.5	25	27.5	30	32.5	35	37.5	%
Percentage of nurse visits to become virtual		7.5	10	12.5	13	13	13	13	13	13	13	%
Probability of a community alarm user being admitted to hospital (%)	32.4	32.2	32	32	32	32	32	32	32	32	32	%
Average duration of a hospital stay for user base	9.5	9	8.75	8.5	8.5	8.5	8.5	8.5	8.5	8.5	8.5	Days
Average additional care visits due to early hospital release (per discharge)		0.8	1.1	1.5	1.5	1.5	1.5	1.5	1.5	1.5	1.5	Visits
Average additional nurse visits due to early hospital release (per discharge)		0.4	0.6	0.9	0.9	0.9	0.9	0.9	0.9	0.9	0.9	Visits
Percentage of people in hospital delayed in discharge – bed blockers	20	18	16	14	12	10	10	10	10	10	10	%
Percentage of people in residential care	3.5	3.38	3.25	3.13	3	3	3	3	3	3	3	%

Financing

Despite the significant potential savings in Table 7.3, if the proposed system is to be introduced it is clear from Table 7.1 that substantial initial borrowing would be required, and this must be included as a cost of the proposed system. For the purpose of analysis the average cost of home-based equipment was set at £700, and it is assumed that finance is available to purchase the current community alarm system with borrowing only required for costs above this system. Assuming then that the loan is paid for out of the proceeds of the project, with an interest rate of 6% there would be £6.4 million outstanding at the end of the first year. It is not until the fifth year that breakeven is achieved and thereafter a positive cash flow secured. Continuing a conservative outlook it is assumed that no interest is gained on

Table 7.3: Operating expenditure in the present and proposed systems

Operating costs (£ x 000)	Present system	Operational year of the proposed telecare system				
		1	3	5	7	10
Forced entry to properties	23	18	18	18	18	18
Unsuccessful carer visits	3	≈0	≈0	≈0	≈0	≈0
Telephone (including control centre, GP/nurse)	14	36	33	34	35	37
GP surgery consultation	413	526	330	336	342	351
GP home visit consultations	383	330	322	314	306	294
Nurse visit (change to virtual consultations)	245	147	143	142	142	142
Hospital bed costs	5,098	4,858	4,618	4,611	4,611	4,611
Residential care	5,603	5,392	4,993	4,793	4,793	4,793
Total	11,783	11,307	10,457	10,248	10,247	10,246

finance after the loan has been repaid. Under these conditions, by the end of the system life cycle, in year 10, there is an accumulated return of the order of £8.3 million compared to the present system, as shown in Figure 7.1.

If this sum were not absorbed elsewhere, this would effectively finance a new replacement system without the need to borrow in the future. The savings with future systems, 10 years hence, would then be even greater as the initial borrowing requirement would be removed and the relatively slow 'take-up' of telecare suggested in Table 7.2 would be replaced with operating levels suggested in year 10 (of Table 7.2). At the end of year 10 it is probable that the proposed

telecare system could be purchased again at a lower price than it would be today. Technology and systems develop, and new enhanced systems would be available and sought after, offering improved functionality and further potential operating savings. Such systems would again be at the cutting edge of technology with an appropriately higher purchase cost.

Figure 7.1 also indicates there is a significant increase in cash flow during year 5. This is due to the community alarm system needing to replace the home-based equipment as its life expectancy is only five years, while the proposed telecare system has an expectancy of 10 years. The cost of replacing the

Figure 7.1: Projected cash flow while paying the loan out of the proceeds of the project

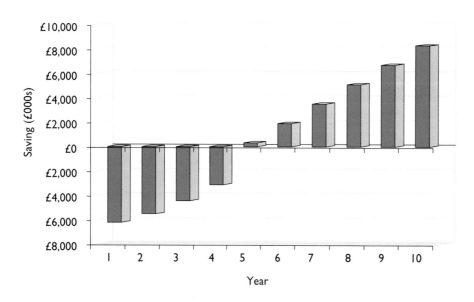

community alarm equipment is approximately £2 million and because it is not evident in the proposed telecare system, is seen as a saving.

Alternative repayment strategies such as paying off the loan over a fixed duration, typically 5 and 10 years, also show that the proposed system is more cost-effective, returning savings of £8.7 million and £7.6 million respectively.

Sensitivity analysis

Mair et al comment that economic evaluations must incorporate a sensitivity analysis (Mair et al, 2000). This allows key areas to be identified and investigated further and therefore provides greater confidence in the results obtained.

Single point analysis

Paying the loan off through the proceeds of the project, that is, as quickly as possible and using the same constraints as discussed above, reveals that at the end of the system life cycle, if the home-based equipment cost £500, a return of £11.3 million is possible. However, when using £1,000 as the home-based equipment cost, this is reduced to an overall return of £3.3 million. If the home equipment cost £1,170 then the community alarm and proposed telecare systems would cost the same to implement as the return from the proposed system approaches zero.

The decision of which system to implement would then be based on the qualitative merits of each system.

Threshold analysis

With such an analysis the model is investigated in order to identify the point at which the conclusions of the model alter, for example, the point at which the proposed telecare system no longer results in financial savings. In this example the home-based equipment is set at £700 and the model investigated in order to discover the service delivery requirements for the system to break even. Figure 7.2 shows that in order for no financial savings to be evident (at a 6% interest rate) the changes described in Table 7.4 must occur. However, these changes are just one of a number of possible scenarios which would result in zero financial savings.

Multiway analysis

A multiway sensitivity analysis involves varying two or more inputs at the same time, and allows greater attention to be drawn to specific areas. The impact of the home equipment cost has a substantial impact in terms of defining the costs of the proposed system, while the two components with the greatest impact on savings are hospital bed and residential care costs. The multiway analysis allows the investigation of these critical savings to be altered at the same time,

Figure 7.2: Cash flows for £700 home equipment cost at different rates of interest

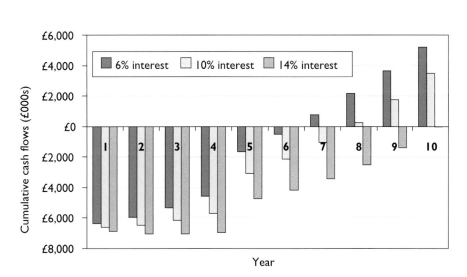

Table 7.4: Assumed saving requirements when the home equipment costs £700

Variables	Present system	Operational year of the proposed telecare system									
		1	2	3	4	5	6	7	8	9	10
Percentage of GP surgery consultations to become virtual		10	12.5	15	17.5	20	22.5	25	25	25	25
Percentage of GP home visit consultations to become virtual		10	12.5	15	17.5	20	22.5	25	25	25	25
Percentage of nurse visits to become virtual		2.5	5	7.5	10	12	12	12	12	12	12
Probability of a community alarm user being admitted to hospital (%)	32.4	32.3	32.2	32.2	32.2	32.2	32.2	32.2	32.2	32.2	32.2
Average duration of a hospital stay for user base	9.5	9	8.75	8.5	8.5	8.5	8.5	8.5	8.5	8.5	8.5
Average additional care visits due to early hospital release (per discharge)		0.8	1.1	1.5	1.5	1.5	1.5	1.5	1.6	1.5	1.5
Average additional nurse visits due to early hospital release (per discharge)		0.4	0.6	0.9	0.9	0.9	0.9	0.9	0.9	0.9	0.9
Percentage of people in hospital delayed in discharge – bed blockers	20	18	16	14	12	10	10	10	10	10	10
Percentage of people in residential care	3.5	3.45	3.40	3.35	3.3	3.25	3.20	3.15	3.1	3.05	3

and in this context, the parameters used in Table 7.2 are again used but with the changes indicated in Table 7.5.

The implications of these service delivery changes are shown in Figure 7.3. The repayment method employed is to pay the loan off through the proceeds of the project, that is, as quickly as possible. Evidently, if the two key variables suggested in Table 7.5 are only 50% as effective, as suggested in Table 7.2, then a surplus of only £2.6 million is available at the end of the system life cycle, some £5.7 million less than that identified in Figure 7.1.

Extreme scenario analysis

This analysis alters the service delivery changes in the expected model (Figure 7.1) to extreme levels, incorporating a pessimistic and optimistic view of the proposed telecare system. Using the home equipment cost of £700 and the key areas in Table 7.2, the optimistic and pessimistic view alter all of the

service delivery changes by 50%. The pessimistic view then returns a saving of £2 million, only £600,000 less than suggested in the multiway sensitivity analysis. (Clearly the service delivery changes excluding hospital and residential care costs make only a slight impact on the system profitability.)

In addition to reducing the service delivery changes by 50%, the model allows the flexibility to increase certain parameters. The results reported above already include an additional GP consultation in the first year of operation due to medical parameters being above GP defined levels. However, it has been suggested that as much as 50% of potential users have medical problems that are currently undiagnosed and could be detected by telecare monitoring (Curry and Norris, 1997). In a worst case scenario, the proposed telecare system may increase the number of GP and nurse consultations. A 50% increase in the number of GP and nurse consultations during the first two years (it is assumed that undiagnosed problems will be detected during this period) lowers the financial

Figure 7.3: Results of multiway sensitivity analysis

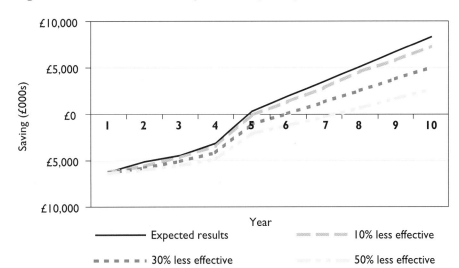

savings to £541,000. A concern over the ability of GPs and nurses to deliver such a dramatic increase in human resources is also worthy of note.

It would seem appropriate that as the pessimistic view decreased the service delivery changes by 50%, that the optimistic model increases them by 50%. The expected results from the model (Table 7.2) indicate a total saving of £8.3 million, while the optimistic view results in a total saving of £14.3 million. It may also be suggested that because the proposed telecare system is a preventative system, detecting medical difficulties earlier than at present, that the number of GP consultations will reduce in the future. It is not thought that there would be a reduction in the number of nurse consultations, as approximately 85%

of consultations require 'hands-on' treatment, for dressing of wounds and so forth (Wootton et al, 1998). Introducing a reduction in GP consultations by 10% for each year in the 10-year system life cycle increases the return still further to £15.2 million.

Discussion

The results from the various sensitivity analyses reveal that under all of the conditions exposed to the proposed telecare system, then for the given assumptions, it is more profitable than the current community alarm system. The exact financial savings are difficult to accurately determine, but would fall within the range indicated by Figure 7.4. In reality

Table 7.5: Multiway sensitivity analysis variables

Effect on service providers of proposed system – community alarm users only		Present system	Operational year of the proposed system					
			1	2	3	4	5 to 10	
Average duration of a hospital stay for user base	Expected model	9.5	9	8.75	8.5	8.5	8.5	Days
	10% less effective	9.5	9.05	8.825	8.6	8.6	8.6	Days
	30% less effective	9.5	9.1	8.975	8.8	8.8	8.8	Days
	50% less effective	9.5	9.25	9.125	9	9	9	Days
% of people in residential care	Expected model	3.5	3.375	3.25	3.125	3	3	%
	10% less effective	3.5	3.3875	3.275	3.1625	3.05	3.05	%
	30% less effective	3.5	3.4125	3.325	3.2375	3.15	3.15	%
	50% less effective	3.5	3.4375	3.375	3.3125	3.25	3.25	%

Figure 7.4: Potential savings with the proposed telecare system

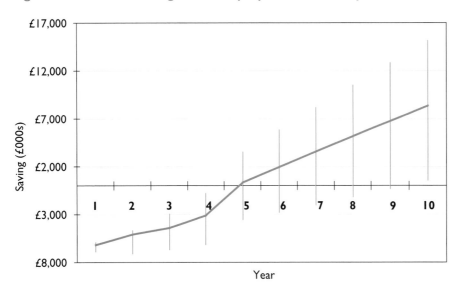

the range is not as significant as suggested by Figure 7.4 as it is unlikely that all of the pessimistic or optimistic factors will occur simultaneously.

The financial implications of telecare systems are not straightforward, with many parties contributing to funding and benefiting from their use. The results from the model suggest that the main savings are to be derived from reduction in time spent in hospital and residential care. Consequently, to realise the full financial rewards, a holistic approach involving collaboration across all imposed service boundaries is an essential pre-requisite. It has been said that:

> ... the general cost-effectiveness of preventing an illness rather than treating it is usually favourable, but the specific cost of the preventive traditionally has to be paid by a party that has not yet incurred the obligation to pay for the illness. Nowhere is this problem more obvious than in the boundaries between hospital, extended care facility and in home care for frail but generally healthy patients. (Loeb, 1999)

The analysis of the proposed telecare system would support this observation. Currently community alarms are funded either privately, through housing benefit, and in a few cases by social services or health. However, the nature of the proposed telecare system suggests that other parties should also contribute to funding as they derive savings from its implementation. Under the expected conditions of

operation (Table 7.2), housing and related care and support budgets, which provide funding in the vast majority of cases, should only contribute 4%, while health budget holders should contribute 47% and residential care 49%. Overall the proposed telecare system requires less finance, but until budget holders can jointly fund such systems, there remains little motivation for separate service providers to innovate and seek developments.

The model suggests that the proposed second generation telecare system saves £8.3 million over a 10-year period when there are 11,618 users. Extrapolating these results to represent the whole country reveals that if all of the 1.6 million community alarm users in the UK were provided with the proposed telecare system, savings in excess of £1 billion would be expected. As identified in Chapter 1, with the increase in the number of older people and therefore potential number of community alarm users, these relative savings could be even greater in further years. A telecare system introduced 10 years after the proposed telecare system could produce even greater savings, as this system would have the infrastructure in place. For example, the percentage of virtual consultations would not need to start at 15% in year 1 and increase to 37.5%; it could start at a high figure from the beginning.

Conclusions

It is a highly complex task to produce a realistic cost-effective model, but the model produced is based on accurate and authoritative figures, typically from government. The results indicate that for the given assumptions, the proposed second generation model is more cost-effective in all analyses and therefore suggests that this is a suitable way forward. However, the model only represents the present community alarm users, who typically have above-average healthcare needs. The evidence is compelling for these users but further work is required to identify other people who would benefit.

Section 3
Implications and recommendations

8

Implications for community alarms

Simon Brownsell and David Bradley

The 1990 NHS and Community Care Act aims to:

> Provide the development of domiciliary care to support people in their own homes and to prevent unnecessary admission to residential care. (DoH, 1992)

The Supporting People proposals go some way to meeting this aim as they seek to provide sole funding for support services. It broadly meets the same support services as those covered by Housing Benefit, but will replace it from April 2003. It will meet 'reasonable charges' for people in supported accommodation since August 1997, and private sector accommodation where the tenant has a valid community care assessment (DETR, 2001).

The introduction of second generation telecare services could be considered as one way of moving towards successful support of people in the community. A consequence of such a shift in emphasis is that hospitals will benefit from a reduced workload as people are maintained more successfully in the community. Conversely, there will be greater demands on staff in the community.

At the centre of the present community alarm system is the control centre (see Figure 2.1) which facilitates appropriate assistance, be that personal care, medical,

emergency or social support. The greater use of technology and sharing of appropriate information between housing, social services and health (with appropriate data gateways and security procedures) will inevitably increase the workload at the control centre. In order to understand this impact a software simulation package has been created using Visual Basic. The simulation allows the present community alarm system to be modelled as well as hypothetical calls anticipated in the second generation telecare system. It is therefore possible to predict the outcomes and understand the impact before changes actually take place.

The present system

With the support of one of the largest community alarm centres in the UK, the present community alarm system has been modelled. Access was granted to the community alarm data and this was used to validate the model, that is, based on actual data and known outcomes the model should reflect what actually happened. Table 8.1 demonstrates the accuracy of the model with the slight differences being explained by the rounding of calls to ensure whole numbers.

Table 8.1: Comparison of the expected and generated number of calls from the model

Month	Real data			Model results		
	Total	System	Operator	Total	System	Operator
6 months	128,510	89,095	39,415	128,291	89,081	39,210

In Table 8.1, system calls refer to any call that does not require operator involvement, such as automatic staff logging on and off duty such as wardens, and routine equipment checks. Operator calls involve the centre operator talking to the caller.

All calls received at the control centre are categorised, for example, if the caller indicates they have fallen, then the category of call will be entered as 'fall'. Each of the categories has an associated average call duration and probability of contacting external services, typically the emergency services, a doctor or responder (warden, carer or family member). Based on accurate actual data indicating when calls are received, their duration, and the occurrence of an outgoing call, it is possible to accurately model the call profile at the control centre.

Based on real shift patterns and call profiles, Table 8.2 indicates the results from the model for the month of June. These figures are based on the historical data from the control centre, with the model introducing a degree of variance to reflect the real world. The number, and type, of calls generated by the model are reflective of the original data; however, the delay (time callers had to wait for an operator to answer their call) is slightly over-estimated in the model. At busy times in the 'real world' additional support from office personnel assist the operators if there is a sudden increase in call volume. However, such a possibility is dependent on 'additional' personnel being available, which is a variable of unknown quantity and has therefore not been included in the model.

When a call is received at the control centre no additional information is given regarding the nature of the call, and therefore calls are answered on a First In First Out (FIFO) basis rather than an order of priority. To ensure an effective service it is therefore necessary to answer all calls as quickly as possible and Table 8.2 indicates that the majority of calls, 97%, are answered without delay. However, calls can quickly become queued and delays introduced. For example, many community alarm control centres function with two operators on duty; if one of these operators has a call requiring significant attention then the remaining operator must answer all of the incoming calls on their own, and a bottleneck can soon materialise.

The control centre in question receives approximately 225 calls requiring the intervention of an operator a day. Investigation of the operators' utilisation rates, an expression which indicates the percentage of time operators were answering calls, reveals that much of the time they are waiting for calls; indeed, rarely does the utilisation figure for a given hour exceed 10%. Therefore, despite the operators having in excess of 90% of their time waiting for calls, because the control centre is so sensitive to calls of any significant length, on occasions callers must wait to be answered. Table 8.3 further reveals the sensitivity of the control centre when the number of calls changes. (The results of Table 8.3 are the average of six simulation runs.)

Increasing the number of operators and number of users should result in improved efficiency without adversely affecting the number of callers who experience delays. The control centre where the original data was obtained from has recognised this, and the community alarm control centre and out-of-hours repair centre have been merged. Using the

Table 8.2: Analysis of the control centre for June

| June | Total | Number of calls | | Delayed | Max delay | Avg delay |
		System	Operator			
1	21,418	14,571	6,847	158	7:43	0:46
2	21,413	14,533	6,880	153	3:52	0:36
3	21,366	14,478	6,888	188	11:45	0:36
4	21,313	14,447	6,866	181	3:30	0:36
5	21,411	14,542	6,869	204	4:17	0:41
6	21,311	14,461	6,850	198	4:37	0:42
Avg	21,372	14,505	6,867	180	5:57	0:40

Table 8.3: Sensitivity of the community alarm control centre to changes in calls during June

Model characteristic	Total	Number of calls		Delayed	Max delay	Avg delay
		System	Operator			
Present system	21,372	14,505	6,867	180	5:57	0:40
20% more sheltered housing schemes	25,719	17,407	8,313	306	11:51	0:50
20% fewer sheltered housing schemes	17,091	11,609	5,482	81	4:36	0:38
15% more community and sheltered housing users	24,656	16,668	7,990	254	9:06	0:51
15% fewer community and sheltered housing users	18,175	12,345	5,830	97	5:04	0:39
Duration of calls increased by 10%	21,365	14,495	6,870	181	7:59	0:46
Duration of calls reduced by 10%	21,332	14,465	6,867	140	6:59	0:47

same shift patterns reveals that the merger results in 5% of calls being delayed for an average of 1.08 minutes. Because delayed repair calls are unlikely to be life threatening, there is the potential to reduce the overall number of operators on duty. For example, if two operators dealt with repair calls and two with community alarm calls prior to the merger, if only three operators were on duty but could answer any type of call then the level of service offered to community alarm users could be improved, although clearly this would be at the expense of the repairs service. After the merger, with an additional 5,000 repair calls per month, reducing the overall number of operator hours even by as much as 36%, reveals that only 17% of calls are delayed for an average of 1.42 minutes.

Modelling a second generation telecare system

For each call type evident in this new generation system the call details have been estimated based on anticipated call profiles and likely technical competency. Table 8.4 reports the results, and it is assumed that all of the users have a second generation system suitable for their needs. The same month and shift pattern as before is applied to enable a like-with-like comparison.

In comparison to the activity of the first generation community alarm centre, as set out in Table 8.2, the second generation system dramatically increases the number of calls received at the control centre. Indeed, for June the overall increase is from 21,372 to 68,617, a 321% increase in call volume. The main reason for the increase is due to the additional monitoring capabilities of the second generation system and the increased volume of data calls, updating the records at the control centre of every user once a week. In the current first generation system it is only usual for sheltered housing main servers to contact the control centre periodically, whereas the second generation system suggests weekly contact between every home (including sheltered housing and community dwellings) and the control centre.

This greater access to information can then be shared between organisations such as the GP, hospital, carer and others. However, only information relevant to each party's particular needs will be accessible to them. The additional access to appropriate information also allows carer packages to be automatically suspended on hospital admission and so on. A further reason for the increased call volume is that the second generation system automatically calls for assistance when the user is unable to do so, a significant improvement in comparison with the technology currently in use.

Table 8.4: Analysis of the second generation system for June

| | Number of calls | | | | | |
	Total	System	Operator	Delayed	Max delay	Avg delay
Present	21,372	14,505	6,867	180	5:57	0:40
Avg (6 runs)	68,617	64,710	3,907	28	3:45	0:38

Even though at first glance Table 8.4 might suggest a dramatic increase in workload, it should be appreciated that the vast majority of the calls refer to greater access to accurate and timely information. As such, these system calls can be dealt with by the system without the need for an operator. Indeed, the model anticipates the number of system calls in the second generation system increases by 446%.

Referring to the first generation system, Table 8.2 indicates that there are 6,867 operator calls for the month of June, while the second generation system receives 3,907 for the same time period, a 57% reduction. So, while the second generation system overall suggests a greater number of calls, the number of calls that require operator response actually reduces. This reduction is primarily achieved by the home-based technology communicating with the alarm user prior to contacting the control centre, giving the user the ability to cancel a call made in error. During June in the first generation system there were 1,874 calls that were made by mistake, and these are effectively removed in the second generation system. The model also assumes that calls regarding security cannot be cancelled (see Table 6.1), to ensure that a burglar, for instance, does not cancel the alarm once they have gained access.

Of more importance than the number of calls answered by the operators is the amount of time spent with callers, and, by implication, the corresponding effect on the number and duration of calls that are delayed. In relation to the first generation system, operators spent 144 hours 46 minutes on calls, while for the second generation system this falls to 79 hours and 11 minutes, a reduction of 55%. Clearly, as less time is required speaking to callers, the operators in the second generation system have more time available to answer calls and this results in a reduction in delayed calls. Indeed, the number of callers who experienced a delay reduces from 180 to 28, while the maximum delay reduces from 5:57 to 3:45 and the average delay,

for those who experienced a delay, reduces from 40 to 38 seconds.

The purpose of this model was to investigate the impact on service delivery at the control centre, and the evidence from the model clearly demonstrates that the second generation can be delivered within the existing service levels. Indeed, the second generation system would seem to reduce the workload on the control centre operators, and therefore improves service delivery, further adding to the evidence for second generation telecare systems to be implemented.

Nevertheless, the second generation system modelled above may not be an accurate reflection of the actual call profiles that could exist when such a system is implemented. It is therefore necessary to perform an extreme scenario analysis. Using Table 8.4 as the anticipated results of the second generation system, Table 8.5 then indicates the results if the number of calls is reduced or increased by 20%. This best and worst case scenario is presented in Table 8.5 as the average of six simulation runs.

The extreme scenario analysis indicates that even if 20% more calls were received than anticipated in the second generation system, then the overall result is that there are still fewer calls delayed in comparison with the first generation system (comparing Table 8.2 and 8.5).

Possible effect on GP workload

The suggested second generation telecare system (Table 6.1) indicated that users would have access to medical monitoring in the home. This monitoring suggests that medical staff will be involved answering the calls generated and therefore it may increase their workload. Because of the medical monitoring equipment, it is suggested that for each user an additional 18.4 minutes of the GP's time will be required in the first year of operation. This is due to

Table 8.5: Extreme scenario analysis of the second generation telecare system for June

	Number of calls					
	Total	**System**	**Operator**	**Delayed**	**Max delay**	**Avg delay**
First generation	*21,372*	*14,505*	*6,867*	*180*	*5:57*	*0:40*
Anticipated second generation	68,617	64,710	3,907	28	3:45	0:38
20% fewer calls	54,924	51,787	3,137	15	3:46	0:47
20% more calls	82,587	77,888	4,698	52	8:49	1:02

an additional consultation of 10.8 minutes for each user falling outside of the medical parameters originally defined by the GP (worst case scenario), together with the 8.4 minutes required to initially define those parameters. The introduction of virtual consultations saves a total of 0.8 minutes per patient in the first year of operation. The 8.4 minutes to initially define user parameters may be included as part of a normal consultation or the annual check up for those aged 75 and over (DoH, 1992).

In subsequent years the proposed system requires slightly less GPs' time than the present system (approximately 1 minute). As indicated in Table 7.2, there will be a growth in the number of consultations that could be performed in the surgery, but the patient chooses to have a virtual consultation instead. This results in a time saving for patients, who do not need the inconvenience of travelling to the GP surgery, but requires slightly more of the GP's time, an additional 2.4[1] minutes to perform the consultation through video conferencing. If these virtual surgery-based GP consultations were not permitted, then compared to the present community alarm system by the fifth year, 3.3 minutes per patient per annum could be saved, this being achieved through an increase in the percentage of virtual home-based consultations suggested in Table 7.2; by the tenth year the potential is for savings in the order of 5 minutes. Clearly such a reduction would be

welcomed by GPs and enable them to spend more time with patients. However, until verified by actual field studies, the results of this analysis must be treated with some caution.

Conclusions

In the past there has been some concern that future telecare enhancements will increase demand on the control centre staff and they will be unable to respond to the anticipated increased call volume. This analysis reveals that the number of calls will indeed increase dramatically by as much as 321%, but many of these calls will not require operator involvement. The actual number of calls that must be responded to reduces by 57%, and likely time savings are anticipated at 55%. Additional information regarding the calls will also allow prioritisation of an emergency call over less significant calls, such as a request for information.

---

[1] Surgery-based consultations are approximately 8.4 minutes while telephone consultations currently require 10.8 minutes (Joint Evidence to the doctors' and dentists' review body from the Health Departments and the General Medical Services Committee, 'General medical practitioners' workload survey 1992-93: final analysis', 1994, p 4). The model assumes that a virtual consultation requires the same time as a telephone consultation.

9

Implications for health and social care

Mark Hawley

The implementation of telecare and the further use of ICTs has the potential to enhance the delivery of health and social care. The evidence presented throughout this report suggests that the time is ripe for the introduction of telecare, but with the caveat that it must be introduced with care, making use of research evidence where available and undergoing a rigorous process of monitoring, evaluation and review as it is introduced. In this way the service user and the service providers will derive maximum benefit from the introduction of these new technologies, while the lessons learnt and pitfalls encountered can be documented for the benefit of others.

Until recently, technological change in the health service has principally been the domain of the acute care sector. The acute sector is subject to 'technology inflation' where it is recognised that new and better technologies will be introduced, and these will inevitably be more expensive. An example of this is the development and introduction of new imaging techniques. Plane film X-ray has been, for some diagnostic purposes, superseded by CT (Computerised Tomography), which has, in turn, been superseded by MRI (Magnetic Resonance Imaging).

Technological change in the primary and community care sector has been nowhere near so rapid, although there are some examples, such as the development of portable ultrasound equipment, that can be used in GPs' surgeries. Another example was the development of environmental control equipment, allowing disabled people to control appliances in their own homes and therefore achieve a greater degree of independence. However, the pace of development of this technology has been slow compared to that in the acute sector.

This situation is now set to fundamentally alter with the rise of ICTs. For the first time, the infrastructure and basic technology is available to give and gather information and to take action remotely. The NHS is currently set up to provide location-based services, that is, services based in institutions. This is done mainly because of economies of scale – it is cost-effective to provide staff and equipment in one location which can be shared by a number of patients. With telecare, the potential exists to deliver services within the home without the need for the physical presence of staff, so that we can now contemplate patient-based, rather than location-based, services. This gives the possibility of an enhanced provision of care in the community and especially in the home of the service user. Crucially, telecare could be available directly within the user's home on a 24-hour basis. The community health and social care services are therefore about to enter a time of rapid technological change. Change cannot be effected solely by the introduction of technology, however, and the main changes that will have to take place are in organisations, services and the funding of services. Effective links and communication between different organisations and services will need to be enhanced, and in particular a holistic approach is required between health, housing and social services.

These changes are likely to have many implications for the service user, the service providers and the funding agencies. The remainder of this chapter suggests some of the implications that may result over the coming years. In so doing it should be appreciated that little published research has been conducted on the impact of telecare or on the structure and process of care (Wallace et al, 1998). *Telecare: New ideas for care and support @ home* (Tang et al, 2000), and other books, have made a useful start, but a more coherent approach is needed. Because second generation telecare systems are not currently available as a commercial product and the support and infrastructure to function correctly is not in place, these thoughts on implications are somewhat tentative and cannot be developed further until telecare has been more fully implemented.

The implications of telecare are potentially huge, and cover the spectrum from technology providers to government. The implications for users to be enabled and empowered to live independently and safely in their own homes are also considerable. This chapter, however, will concentrate principally on the implications for the NHS and its immediate partner organisations (social services and housing) as, in the delivery of telecare, these organisations will be responsible for its success or failure.

Organisational issues

Health services are examining their practices to try to reduce the number of older people who are in hospital beds inappropriately. The 'National Service Framework for Older People' (DoH, 2001b) introduced the concept of intermediate care. Telecare can be seen as one of the possible ways of providing intermediate care. It is clear that people are admitted to institutional settings for a range of reasons, and these are often a complex interaction between health, social, personal and possibly economic factors. If we wish to use technology to help people to remain in their own homes, the technology will have to address a range of factors and not simply ones that fit neatly into the category of 'health', 'housing' or 'social care'. This will have implications regarding the range of technology that should be made available but most importantly will have implications on the way that services are organised to provide, maintain and respond to the technology.

In deciding whether to discharge someone from hospital, health and social care staff examine the medical, nursing, social care needs, and housing suitability of the individual. A decision not to discharge can be taken for reasons of continuing need

for medical care or monitoring, or because nursing or social care (including informal carer support) is not available in the person's home. Earlier chapters have examined the ways in which telecare can be used to assist early discharge from hospital. In many cases, telecare may be a means of addressing both the medical and social care needs of the individual. This reinforces the argument that telecare facilitates person-centred services and does not fit neatly into the still wide, though closing, health/social divide.

One of the challenges posed by telecare is how best to organise services such that people are enabled to stay in their own homes. Two of the major elements of service provision around telecare are how to handle data and alerts from the telecare systems, and how to respond to adverse conditions, such as alarms. A possible model is shown in Figure 9.1. At the heart is the client in their own home, or in an intermediate care setting for a period of rehabilitation. They are provided with the telecare system and modules (defined in Chapter 6) that meet their specific needs, along with a community care package if appropriate.

The key to this system is communication and information exchange between the user's home and the service contact points. Figure 9.1 suggests that the two main contact points, acting as gatekeepers, could be the community alarm control centre and NHS Direct. The route taken is dependent on the type of assistance required; if it is clear that medical assistance is required then NHS Direct would be contacted, whereas for all other types of call the community alarm would be more appropriate. Despite the distinction between these, there is some commonality and possibly re-routing of calls between them. There could also be some scope for merger, as is already evident where at least one NHS Direct site has taken over the responsibilities of a local community alarm centre.

When action needs to be taken, the community alarm control centre can contact anyone with a telephone through the PSTN (Public Switched Telephone Network). In addition to contact via the telephone system, NHS Direct can also connect to the NHS' own network NHSNet. Here access to medical data and the EPR may be achievable, along with the sending of images and data to medical practitioners, if necessary, for remote consultation. Telecare systems will need to link with the EPR.

Figure 9.1: A possible systems approach to providing telecare

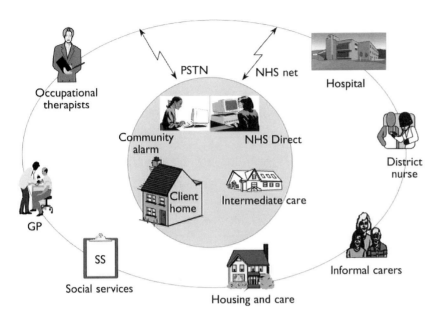

This information, with the addition of that available from the telecare sensors and monitoring in the home, will provide considerable information to key personnel when assessments and evaluations are required.

Figure 9.1 also indicates the main sources of support available from the community alarm control centre and NHS Direct site. Further details on the structure and communication paths can be found elsewhere (Williams et al, 1999).

In order to operate this type of system, and to respond appropriately to alerts and alarms from a telecare system, it is clear that services will have to work together in a much more coherent and timely manner than is currently the case. Figure 9.1 makes little distinction between health and social care, and also involves housing providers and informal carers. The system will require that information is available to all the parties involved (although for security purposes the level of access to this information must be controlled), and that rapid communication, through voice or data networks, is available. This will demand that the information systems of these various providers work together and share appropriate data in real time. The system will need to be controlled by a robust set of agreed protocols, which set out the response to different situations and the information

available to which people under what circumstances. All of this will need to be agreed with the client.

Chapter 3 indicated that recent government policy has been designed to reduce the gap between health, social care and housing. This appears to be progressing, although at different speeds in different locations. The introduction of telecare will require a high level of integration between different services; the key will be to put in place the services required around the individual.

Investment and funding

To be at its most effective, telecare requires that, with appropriate security, patient information is freely accessible throughout the care system. The UK government is currently spending more on information technology (IT) than ever before and in 2002, NHS spending on IT will top £1 billion for the first time. However, this represents only about 2% of the NHS budget, and therefore investment in IT remains low in comparison with other industries and the average expenditure on IT in the government as a whole (Ranger, 2002).

The investment needed to implement telecare will be considerable. Chapter 7 suggests that for a system where the home-based equipment costs £700 that this would result in an initial investment, for a city the size of Birmingham, of £6.4 million. The possible cost savings, as modelled in Chapter 7, are then attributed to the various agencies as follows: NHS – 47%; housing services – 4%; residential care – 49%. This suggests that the greatest savings are to be gained in health and social services provision, and it would therefore appear logical that the major investment in telecare should be made jointly by health and social services, with input from housing services.

Some money has been made available by the government for community equipment, which includes telecare equipment, to be spent on the joint provision of health and social services, although there is little evidence that this funding has actually been used to fund telecare. Realistically, in order for investment to take place in telecare, disinvestment will be needed in other services. For strategic health authorities and trusts to take this decision, the evidence base in support of telecare will need to be considerably better than it is currently.

If telecare can be used to support people in their own homes and to enable them to call for assistance when appropriate, then there is inevitably a need to support users in their own homes. Telecare technology of itself is of limited use if the heating system in the house is not sufficient, and the older person becomes at risk of hypothermia. Physical improvements to the property, along with care and repair schemes (such as the Anchor 'Staying Put' scheme), are as important as telecare if the heart of the issue is in enabling the person to remain in their own home with a high level of quality of life. All of these costs will have to be taken into account when future investment in home care, with the aid of telecare, is being considered.

Despite the required level of investment, there is some evidence to suggest that telecare will lead to savings in expenditure on health and social care (Iakovidis and Balas, 1999; Tang et al, 2000; Brownsell et al, 2001), although this is not universally agreed.

Research and development

The evidence base for telecare is currently fairly sparse. Although there has been some work on the feasibility of telecare and the development of the technology (Curry and Norris, 1997), there has been little evaluation of the delivery of telecare in a real setting. There is a dilemma in the introduction of any new technology or service, in that before it is introduced the evidence base should be there to support it, whereas it is difficult to build the evidence base if the service has not been introduced – at least on a pilot basis in a few locations. The accumulation of the evidence base is also a lengthy process, and to prove the efficacy and efficiency of a new technology or service can easily take five years.

There is a need, therefore, to introduce telecare carefully. Certain districts within the UK have already taken a lead in the introduction of telecare (for example, Durham and West Lothian). It is important that the introduction of telecare in these districts is fully evaluated from an efficacy and cost-effectiveness point of view. Any further districts that decide to introduce telecare, in the light of the existing favourable, although scarce, evidence, should also be prepared to resource a rigorous programme of evaluation to accompany the introduction of the telecare service, and to disseminate the results widely.

A number of key activities within the provision of telecare are in need of research. These are:

- development of new telecare technologies;
- human factors involved in telecare design;
- user perspectives in telecare (for example, acceptability, ethics and so on);
- development of the most effective means of assessment for telecare;
- assessment of efficacy, efficiency and cost-effectiveness of telecare interventions;
- service delivery and organisation related to telecare services.

Because of the potential impact of telecare on health and social services, and on the well-being of older people, the Department of Health (through its large-scale various research programmes) and the research councils and charities should have an interest in providing funding for large-scale research projects. Funding may also be forthcoming from companies producing telecare equipment, as they will wish to provide evidence to support the introduction of this technology.

Staff issues: training and development

Telecare is a new area for service providers and there are questions as to whether adequate skills are available within the relevant organisations, as the application of telecare can require both clinical skills as well as skills and knowledge in technology. In the supply of telecare services, one group of professionals who have the requisite skills and training for assessment and provision of complex electronic assistive technologies are clinical scientists working within Medical Physics, Clinical Engineering or Bio-engineering departments in the NHS. The Department of Health has recognised the potential contribution that clinical scientists could make in the introduction of this technology (DoH, 2001c). It is important that these clinical scientists are supported within departments that already have a community role in the assessment and provision of electronic assistive technology, such as environmental control systems. Other professions will also have a key role in the provision of telecare, especially occupational therapists and community nurses. There will clearly be training requirements for these staff, and this training is likely to be an important part of the role of the clinical scientist. Newly available postgraduate courses in assistive technology, which are open to clinical or technological disciplines, may provide appropriate training for professionals taking on these tasks.

Elsewhere, training may be required to support the community alarm control centre staff who traditionally are situated in housing. How they prioritise calls and respond to circumstances will all require careful planning and training. There are implications for sheltered housing and new build properties, as to what infrastructure needs to be in place to ensure the dwellings are future proof, for example, the data requirements of cabling between homes, placement of sensors and power/communication sockets and so on.

The change in emphasis away from hospital and residential care towards home care will probably lead to an increase in community-based staff. In the example of early discharge with telecare, technical personnel may be required to install equipment and provide user training. Community nurse visits may be required during recuperation, while additional home help may also be required. To achieve this, sufficient human resources must be available, or early discharge cannot be realised.

It has already been mentioned that primary and social care is likely to experience a greater demand on its resources and that a re-emphasis of resources may be required from the acute sector in order to deliver services to people in their own homes. Alongside this, GP practices are also likely to experience a change in their workload. Chapter 6 defined the generations of telecare technology, and indicated that video conferencing would become part of service delivery. This could result in travel time savings for home visits, but the automatic generation of alert calls, when the telecare monitoring equipment in the home indicates that medical attention may be required, will create a new type of GP consultation. Chapter 8 indicated that, overall, telecare would result in some time savings for the GP, but further investigation is required when systems are more widespread.

Support to these front-line workers must also be available on demand. For example, if a community nurse requires additional support or a second opinion then, either by telephone, video conference or 3G mobile phone (enabling video conferencing), this assistance should be provided while the healthcare professional is in the patient's home. Such a possibility may also be beneficial to a GP where they could request assistance from a consultant or Accident and Emergency doctor. NHS Direct could facilitate some of this additional 'on-demand' support, providing access to nurses and doctors. This may also, however, imply a change in role for the hospital doctor, who may be required to spend some time on call for video consultation.

The additional information from the EPR and telecare sensors in the home is only beneficial to front-line staff if they can easily obtain the information relevant for their needs. Over recent years considerable efforts have been made at enhancing the human computer interface to make such systems user friendly. Nevertheless, staff training will be required and the acceptance of telecare systems by professionals will require a considerable cultural change. The preceding chapters have indicated the potential of telecare and it is hoped that, with appropriate training, it will be embraced by professionals.

The shift towards self-management

Telecare is expected to lead to a shift in the relationship between the service user and the service provider. The service user's role should be empowered by the new technology for a number of reasons. The first of these is the availability of more and higher quality information. There has already been, in recent years, a shift in the balance of power between doctors and patients (Canter, 2001). Patients are able to access huge quantities of information on the Internet about their health and the diseases from which they suffer. As mentioned in Chapter 1, many doctors have experienced the patient who arrives for a consultation with a wad of printed sheets, downloaded from the Internet, and who can discuss their management on more equal terms with the doctor because they are better informed. It is now recognised that self-management is an important element of, and sometimes the most effective means of, dealing with chronic illness. The information intervention has become just as important as medication in the treatment of some chronic conditions such as rheumatoid arthritis (Branch et al, 1999).

Access to better information will also include, in the future, information about local services and guidelines for their access. Through the Internet or interactive digital TV a patient will be able to find out what services are available to them and therefore be better informed about their rights.

Another reason for the shift in the relationship between service user and service provider will be the location of the provision. A patient going into hospital is in foreign territory and is thus at a disadvantage compared to the staff, who are on familiar ground. This is reversed when service users are increasingly on their own home ground (that is, at home), and it is the service providers who are in foreign territory.

It is thus to be expected that the service user will exercise their right to appropriate care and treatment as more of an equal partner with the service provider. A consequence of this is that the service user will also be encouraged to take greater responsibility for their own care; as stated above, self-management is an effective healthcare strategy.

Conclusions

It is difficult to foresee the kind and extent of changes that could result if telecare were implemented on a large scale. Telecare and ICT clearly have considerable potential across many different aspects of health and social care. In addressing the second and subsequent generations of telecare vision laid down in Chapter 6, this chapter has attempted to indicate the possible implications. The implications for organisations and personnel are considerable. The divide between health, housing and social care will have to close for telecare to succeed, and personnel will need to learn new skills and new ways of working.

It is evident that initially a greater degree of resources will be necessary in primary and social care, and that a great reliance will be placed on computing and information access. However, perhaps the greatest implication is that, if successful, telecare could assist many older and disabled people to live safely and independently in their own homes for longer. If this can be achieved, and as indicated previously there is evidence that such a system is wanted by users and that it is cost-effective and deliverable, then the implications for service providers should be outweighed by the benefits and potential long-term savings that could be derived by introducing such systems.

10

Conclusions and recommendations

Simon Brownsell and David Bradley

The emphasis in this report has been on the identification of the benefits of telecare and the ability of technology-based systems to support older and/or disabled people in the community. The subject of telecare has been introduced and the reasons why technology is being investigated highlighted. These can be summarised as:

- the current support and care system has difficulty meeting the demands made on it. An intensive service is being delivered where greater amounts of assistance are provided to a smaller number of people;
- the UK and much of the 'developed' world are facing a situation where the numbers of older people are expected to increase dramatically. The EU has predicted that between 1995 and 2025 the UK will see a 43.6% increase in the 60 and over age range (*The Guardian*, 5 March 1996);
- the majority of people who need support would prefer to stay in their own homes for as long as possible with this being reflected in government policy;
- older people absorb the greatest amounts of care and also the greatest proportion of hospital resources;
- older people already use technology to aid their independence and the Royal Commission for Long-Term Care expects older people in future to be as comfortable with computer controls as the present generation are with telephones;
- the community alarm system is used by approximately 1.6 million users in the UK and may be regarded as an under-utilised resource.

This report has sought to inform policy makers and developers of the real opportunities that exist in the provision of a cost-effective health, care, and support mechanism for older people in their own homes. Government and health-related policies have recently sought to stimulate this field, in particular with the £105 million Community Equipment services funding, yet there is still relatively little research to indicate what form telecare should take, what is required, and how effective it might be. Throughout this report answers to these questions have been sought and in order to maximise cost-effectiveness it is suggested that the community alarm system is used as a starting point for developments.

There are approximately 1.6 million community alarm users in the UK, and these people typically have above average healthcare needs; therefore there is the opportunity for real benefits to users while reducing overall costs. They already use technology to aid their independence and safety while, as Chapter 5 revealed, they are receptive to advances in technology. Based on the views of users and providers, it is possible to indicate the kinds of systems and technologies that may be evident in years to come. Tests can then be applied to these systems to indicate if they could be successful. The views of users and providers indicated that a second generation telecare system would be welcomed, while the tests applied to the telecare systems envisaged in the future also yielded positive results.

How cost-effective telecare might be is a fundamental question that has remained largely unanswered. Chapter 7 suggests that it is possible that the total spend over its lifetime, when considering 11,600 users in a city such as Birmingham, UK, over a 10-year period, of the proposed second generation telecare system, is £8.3 million less than the present community alarm system. Nationally this suggests a possible saving of approximately £100 million per year. Telecare also has the potential to assist other user groups, such as the post-acute care of patients with chronic heart failure and COPD (Chronic Obstructive Pulmonary Disease) as has been demonstrated recently in Yorkshire. Here patients are discharged from hospital early and receive support and monitoring in the community.

Attention has also been given to service delivery implications and the impact that a second generation telecare system could have on these. The results of extensive modelling have indicated that the control centre, the current central point of the community alarm system, can cope with the increased volume of calls produced. Indeed, the actual time spent answering calls is reduced by 55% due to the improved effectiveness and efficiency of the proposed second generation telecare system. Telecare therefore has the potential to:

• be welcomed, indeed driven by users;
• be welcomed by service providers;
• require slightly less control centre operator and GP time, while reductions may also be evident for carers, and hospital admission/discharge staff;
• require less finance than the present community alarm system.

However, while there is undoubtedly the possibility for significant improvements in health, care, and support mechanisms, there will be a cost to pay if these benefits are to be realised. Perhaps the greatest challenges are the change in healthcare emphasis, away from hospitals to a greater emphasis on care and support in the community, and technology opposition by key personnel who deliver care. While there are some technology obstacles to overcome it is believed that these are secondary and can be overcome relatively easily in comparison.

Although the main emphasis has been on the positive aspects of telecare, suggesting that such a facility should be provided to enable people greater levels of choice and the ability of users to stay in their own homes, there are some aspects to telecare that are less positive and could be problematic if not dealt with sensitively.

Ethical considerations

The issue of gaining consent with dementia users may be at the more extreme end of ethical consideration, but even a standard telecare system with sensors distributed throughout the home or worn on the body measuring behaviour patterns and health raises ethical issues. It may be suggested that there are two levels to consider.

Level 1: the fundamental ethical question

Perhaps the fundamental issue, which is rarely discussed, is should this type of monitoring be provided? Should society seek a solution where older people are enabled in the community through the use of technology? Should society be looking to provide more 'hands-on care', should care be provided in people's homes or in the form of residential care? There has been much academic debate over many years regarding what is successful ageing. Over time, various theories have been discussed, ranging from the disengagement theory, where to disengage from society as you become older is considered normal behaviour, to the activist theory, where the reverse is true, and where to disengage from society is considered abnormal.

Telecare is a tool, and consequently in certain circumstances it is a suitable aid and in others it may not be appropriate. It does, however, provide more choice and will provide certain people with the ability to stay in the community with a higher level of independence. It is also noteworthy that surveys of older people indicated that they welcomed such possibilities.

Level 2: the ethics of empowerment

At this level the issue concentrates on how the user interacts with the technology and how they should be in control of it. The second generation telecare system discussed in this report seeks to put the user in control by providing a cancel function on alert calls. Therefore, when outside of agreed parameters, the user is asked whether external contact should be made; only if no response is obtained will support be sought.

This level also includes the freedom of information outside of the house. Various strategies have been discussed and tested, that is, sending all of the data periodically to a central computer for analysis, or analysing the data in the home and only contacting external resources when assistance is required. This latter approach may be deemed ethically more acceptable as the detection of alert situations occurs in real time, rather than waiting for analysis at some pre-defined time.

However, it may be suggested that there is an ethical argument to develop telecare systems. People are choosing to stay living independently in their own homes for as long as possible and telecare could enable this while providing greater levels of security and increasing levels of well-being.

Intrusion

There is some evidence to suggest that some community alarm users consider themselves as more, rather than less, vulnerable because of the service (Thornton and Moutain, 1992) and for these people the perceived benefits are not sufficient enough to outweigh the feeling of intrusion. However, it has been suggested that telecare systems can be acceptable if the following issues are addressed (Fisk, 1996):

Attitude to technology: users must not regard new hardware as a sign of dependency, that is, a badge of dependency or disability.

Promotion and marketing: attention should be given to the positive aspects of new devices and technologies rather than on negative associations of fear, anxiety, falls and so forth.

Aesthetic design: reducing the visibility of the equipment to the point where it blends into the background or can be hidden.

User empowerment: ensuring that control over the transmission of data outside of the home rests in the hands of the user.

Automatic operation: limiting the need for the user to interact with the equipment so that it appears less intrusive.

It is also noteworthy that the Anchor/British Telecom telecare trial indicated that users were concerned that the technology was intrusive before the study commenced, but by the end of the trial only 13% considered it 'slightly intrusive'. If efforts are made to reduce the size of the sensors and other technologies, and the system functions in a way where the user is in control, then it may be that fears of intrusion are not as big an obstacle as might be suggested by some professionals.

Legal considerations

The legal aspects of telecare and assistive technology form a large and growing subject area and will only be mentioned briefly here. Perhaps one of the reasons why the take-up of telecare has been relatively slow is that the legal position of telecare is not clear. Questions must be asked regarding the legal position; for example, if someone is wearing a fall detection unit on their hip, falls over and claims the reason they broke their hip was because of their landing on the fall detector. It would not appear that any legal precedent exists for this. Consider also the case with remote teleconsultations. What is the legal position if someone claims they would have been diagnosed better if they had received a physical consultation rather than a remote video based consultation? Such questions need to be asked and must be considered in any delivery of telecare systems.

Despite the uncertainty around such questions it should be appreciated that the present system is also open to such uncertainty. For example, what are the legal implications if the community alarm fails to function properly or (with the exception of negligence) if a doctor fails to take the most appropriate cause of action? The use of email may pose a further question but is this really any different to telephone advice by NHS Direct? The use of the Internet has also been questioned, with patients having greater access to information that may then be used to self-diagnose or take to their GP. But information was always available in libraries and books. Such technologies just open new ways of communicating and choice to users; the challenge is to embrace them so that users and providers benefit.

Additional information on this area can be found in the Green Paper *Legal aspects of health telematics*, published by the European Health Telematics Association and available at www.ehtel.org.

Recommendations

In the light of the above, it should be evident that telecare and assistive technologies in general could increase the independence, safety and security of older and/or disabled people in their own homes. As society ages and the number of people in need of assistance living in the community grows, there is a real challenge to be met, and the greater use of technology could be part of the answer. There are hurdles to overcome as with any new developments, but the potential benefits for all parties is considerable, and real efforts are being made to embrace the opportunity. For telecare to flourish a number of recommendations are suggested for various parties in the belief that if these can be met, users will have greater levels of choice and the ability to improve their quality of life.

Academia

Greater evidence is needed regarding two key areas: user requirements and cost-effectiveness. Academia also should play a greater role in informing policy makers, stimulating debate and evaluation of the larger trials beginning to take place. Various initiatives are becoming evident such as the NCAR (National Collaboration on Ageing Research, www.shef.ac.uk/ukncar), the GO Programme (Growing Older Programme, www.shef.ac.uk/uni/projects/gop) and EQUAL Initiative (Extending Quality Life, 'Prolonging independence in old age, www.fp.rdg.ac.uk/equal).

Acute hospital care

This could be a major winner as patients are delayed in entering hospital and are discharged earlier. However, rapid response teams, community services and intermediate care must work closely to deliver a healthcare system that meets the patients' needs irrespective of physical location. Particular attention should be given to the discharging of patients to enable appropriate care and support when re-entering the community.

British Standards Organisation (BSO)

There is a requirement for communication protocols to be defined so that manufacturers can produce sensors knowing that their sensors can work with other suppliers' equipment. This also allows commissioners to purchase sensors that best meet the needs of the user, rather than having to buy all of the sensors from one manufacturer. This also allows smaller companies to produce innovative sensors knowing that these will work with standard equipment in common use.

The BSO could also have a role to play in providing some form of quality assurance mark. Therefore, any telecare device with this mark would be known to function to an appropriate standard. This would therefore help to reduce the risk of people purchasing telecare systems that do not function as suggested. As part of this quality assurance mark, attention could be given to particular devices, that is, fall detectors, to state and verify how effective such a device must be.

Community alarm control centres

The analysis of the control centre in this report has indicated that control centres may be regarded as under-utilised. For political reasons, councils may keep their community alarm control centres but, under Supporting People arrangements, and in order to offer a 'Best Value service', their role must expand to offer other services. For example, out-of-hours repairs, first point of contact for all council services, outgoing calls and reassurance to community alarm users, and so on. If the role does not expand then NHS Direct are well positioned to absorb the service and this has already happened in at least one NHS Direct site.

Community Equipment services

The announcement of the £105 million for Community Equipment services (DoH, 2001c) funding provides a real opportunity to stimulate the telecare field and provide funding for new technology and systems. Indeed the guide to integrating Community Equipment services comments that the new investment may be used to "… improve the range of products available, including modular telecare information and communication technologies".

However, efforts must be made to ensure that this 'new money' is not used solely to fund existing services or to meet budget short falls. The opportunity exists to stimulate the market and demand telecare services that meet user need. The Community Equipment services review panel must seek to ensure that the aim of increasing the range of products available is actually met.

Fall clinics

Greater emphasis has been placed on the prevention and rehabilitation of people who have fallen since the introduction of the National Service Framework for Older People (DoH, 2001a). The occurrence of a fall and appropriate investigation may result in a telecare system being implemented. Clinicians must be aware of the technology and systems available, not just regarding telecare but also Environmental Control Systems and other assistive technologies that may enable people to live independently and safely in the community.

Government

While government policy supports telecare and much has been achieved recently regarding the bringing together of health, social services and housing, vertical funding streams can make telecare solutions complex. Older people's needs are often complex and the funding mechanisms do not always support cross-budget funding. A holistic approach is required and attention must be given to the funding links with NHS Direct, both for early hospital discharge and also for the continual monitoring of patients.

Home Improvement Agencies

Alongside social services and assessors, Home Improvement Agencies are well placed to monitor installation contracts and to ensure people who wish to remain in their own home have the technology infrastructure to be able to do so.

Housing services providers

Within both the private and public sector, there is a need to work with manufacturers and to ensure that developments meet user needs and service provider requirements. Telecare also suggests new ways of interacting with services, for example, through the use of email. Housing providers should seek to ensure that they provide users with access choices and

ensure that the quality of the service provided does not depend on the access method chosen. Embracing new communication methods also provides new opportunities for disabled and non-English speaking users.

Intermediate care

As outlined in Standard Three of the National Service Framework, this could be a key component of any telecare system, bridging the gap between hospital and home. There is therefore the opportunity for comprehensive assessment and provision as necessary. As developments in intermediate care take place, the greater use of telecare systems should be investigated to bridge the gap further and provide assistance to people in their own homes.

NHS Direct

A pivotal role can be played by NHS Direct. They are uniquely placed to respond to medical problems in the community and to facilitate early hospital discharge as they can provide monitoring of patients in their own home. A telecare group has recently been formed by NHS Direct and this group must seek to foster links both within health, to allow early discharge, but also with organisations in the community, to avoid hospital admission or a move 'up the care ladder'. They also have a role to play in specifying how they want the telecare systems to work due to their size and potential organisational strength. Telecare also offers the opportunity for income generation at NHS Direct sites.

Older people

Many older people are already using technology to assist them in their daily living and to increase their level of independence and security in the home. Older people need to become more proactive in their pursuit of assistive technologies and telecare. Particular emphasis needs to be placed on skills development, training and education, especially around the Internet (perhaps for web-based shopping) and email.

Primary Care Trusts (PCTs)

Over the coming years PCTs are likely to become the key commissioners of telecare services to local people. They should therefore ensure that they are aware of telecare and technological developments and make every effort to ensure that funding mechanisms are in place. PCTs also have the ability to influence what developments take place as they will decide what can be purchased and offered to local people. Their role is therefore very important and they must seek to understand the opportunities of telecare systems and services.

Residential care/nursing care

Telecare systems could be used to provide greater levels of dignity and independence to residents. Fall detection, incontinence monitoring, and electronic tagging for people with dementia could all be beneficial. Sensors that detect when a user is out of their bed may also be beneficial for some people, therefore replacing a physical 30/60 minute check by staff that may be considered intrusive. Residential and nursing staff must take a more active role in defining their requirements and using the technology to increase the level of independence offered to residents.

Sheltered housing

One of the largest user groups of the present first generation telecare system is sheltered housing, and therefore they are likely to be equally significant in the development and early introduction of second generation systems. Housing providers, including community alarm control centres, need to make greater efforts to understand their clients' wishes and to seek developments that support the residents they serve. The role of the warden cannot be underestimated. Their knowledge of users must be incorporated into system and technology development. Sheltered housing has the opportunity to be at the forefront of developments as users are geographically in one location; however, to date they have been slow to embrace the opportunity.

Social services departments/occupational therapists/clinical engineers

Social services departments, occupational therapists and clinical engineers need to embrace the opportunities and may have to take on an assessment role if telecare and its running costs are to be publicly funded. Understanding what the technology can and cannot do is an important role that must be addressed as they act as gatekeepers and decision makers on what telecare systems are prescribed to users.

Supporting People

The new funding systems for low level support in the community from April 2003 affords an opportunity for community alarms and telecare to demonstrate their cost-effectiveness in facilitating people to remain independent. Conversely commissioners could remove funding from community alarms and redirect it to other services seeking to help people in the community. Hence, there is a real urgency to demonstrate the benefits and cost-effectiveness of telecare.

Technology providers (community alarm providers)

The present community alarm equipment is technically fairly simplistic and companies have been slow to seek technical developments. Historically this has been because the funding mechanisms for purchasers have not been in place and therefore only a limited market existed for emerging products. However, this is now changing and companies need to embrace the opportunities.

It is also recommended that more research be conducted to prove the reliability and accuracy of devices. For example, many of the community alarm providers supply fall detectors but how accurate are they, are there any types of falls that cannot be detected, what are the risks of wearing the device, possibilities for false alarms and so on? Research is also required to suggest appropriate user groups and to indicate likely cost savings. If there is evidence to prove the technology is beneficial then this will not only help users but increase sales and develop the market.

Further, 'plug-and-play' systems are required so that commissioners have the ability to use sensors from different manufacturers which best meet the users' needs rather than being 'tied in' with one manufacturers. There is therefore a requirement for manufacturers to work with one another and in particular the British Standards Organisation (BSO) to define the protocols and communication paths that allow a truly 'plug-and-play' type system to the user.

Final thought

Telecare is an emerging discipline that really could be an *all win*. Users benefit by being enabled to stay in their own home for longer; the healthcare system benefits by acting in a preventative way and enabling early hospital discharge; government benefits by reduced overall spend; and therefore everyone benefits as taxes are used more efficiently. Finally we would agree with the recent Health Select Committee recommendations on telecare, as stated in the report on delayed hospital discharges (2002):

> Telemedicine and telecare solutions, as well as offering alternatives to residential care will enable people to remain at home safely for longer....

> We believe that telecare solutions have a major contribution to make as part of the strategy for developing alternatives to hospitalisation. This is an area in which health, social services, and other local authority services all have an interest, and where there is scope for pooling budgets to develop strategies. We recommend that the Department should establish a national strategy to promote the systematic development of telecare solutions as part of the spectrum of care at home....

> Telecare has the potential not only to achieve cost savings, particularly in the management of acute conditions, but also to be a key component in the drive to allow people the choice of staying longer in their own homes. An additional benefit is that patient autonomy will be increased in that patients will play a more active role in managing their own conditions. We believe that the Government should examine ways of facilitating greater uptake of telecare solutions within both health and social care. In particular it is essential that primary care trusts have the expertise to engage creatively with these technologies, and that local authorities are aware of the possibilities afforded by technology....

References

Advisor on Informatics of the WHO (World Health Organisation) (1997) *Report by the WHO Director General to the 99th Session of the Executive Board*, Ref: EB99/30, Geneva: WHO.

Age Concern (2001) www.ageconcern.org.uk/ageconcern/staying-427.htm.

Alber, J. (1993) 'Health and social services: summarised from older people in Europe: social and economic policies', *Ageing International*, vol XX, no 4, pp 15-19.

Allen, A., Roman, L., Cox, R. and Cardwell, B. (1996) 'Home health visits using a cable television network: user satisfaction', *Journal of Telemedicine and Telecare*, vol 2, no 1, pp 92-4.

Allen, A., Doolittle, C.G., Boysen, D.C., Komoroski, K., Wolf, M., Collins, B. and Petterson, D.J. (1999) 'An analysis of the suitability of home health visits for telemedicine', *Journal of Telemedicine and Telecare*, vol 5, pp 90-6.

Anonymous (1997) 'Classic episodes in telemedicine', *Journal of Telemedicine and Telecare*, vol 3, p 233.

ASAP (Association of Social Alarm Providers) (1997) *ASAP newsletter*, p 7.

Ashton, G. (1997) 'The legal dilemmas of risk and restraint', *Exchange on Ageing Law and Ethics*, vol 5, p 8.

Attwater, D.J. and Whittaker, S.J. (1996) Interactive speech systems for telecommunications applications', *BT Technology Journal*, vol 14, no 2, pp 11-23.

Barnes, N.M., Edwards, N.H., Rose, D.A.D. and Garner, P. (1998) 'Lifestyle monitoring: technology for supported independence', *IEE Computing and Control Engineering Journal*, vol 9, no 4, pp 169-74.

Barnes, N., Collier, G., Cook, S., Ellis, M., Halls, J.A.T., Hill, N., Turton, P. and Wolff, H.S.W. (2000) 'Millennium Homes: a technology supported environment for frail and elderly people', Proceedings of the 6th Annual National Conference of the Institute of Physics and Engineering in Medicine, Southampton, 12-14 September.

Bashshur, R. and Lovett, J. (1977) 'Assessment of telemedicine: results of the initial experience', *Aviation, Space and Environmental Medicine*, vol 48, pp 65-70.

Bassnett, V. (2001) 'High-tech home offers freedom on command', *Barnsley Chronicle*, 16 February, p 17.

BBC News (1998a) 'Social services face acute cash shortage' (http://news.bbc.co.uk/1/health/119224.stm), 24 June.

BBC News (1998b) 'NHS set for IT revolution' (http://news.bbc.co.uk/1/hi/health/179024.stm), 24 September.

Berlo, A. (1999) 'International conference on smart homes and telematics', Program abstracts, p 1.

Bjørneby, S. (1997) 'Using technology in houses for people with dementia', The BESTA flats in Tonsberg, Human Factors Solutions.

Bloomberg Money (2000) 'Silver surfers make net gains' (www.annuity-bureau.co.uk/pub-silver-surfers.html), December.

Boothroyd, D. (1997) 'Mind over matter', *New Electronics on Campus*, pp 6-8.

Bradley, D.A., Williams, G., Brownsell, S. and Levy, S. (2002) 'Community alarms to telecare: a system strategy for an integrated telehealth provision', *Technology and Disability*, vol 14, no 2, pp 63-74.

Branch, H.K., Lipsky, K., Nieman, T. and Lipsky, P.E. (1999) 'Positive impact of an intervention by arthritis patient educators on knowledge and satisfaction of patients in a rheumatology practice', *Arthritis Care and Research*, vol 12, no 6, pp 370-5.

Brodie-Smith, A. (1993) 'A grey area: a critical deconstruction of the burden of elderly people', *Generations Review*, vol 3, no 2, pp 6-8.

Bronzino, J.D., Morelli, R.A. and Goethe, J.W. (1995) 'An expert system for monitoring psychiatric treatment', *IEEE Engineering in Medicine and Biology Magazine (EMBS)*, vol 14, no 6, pp 776-80.

Brownsell, S., Bradley, D.A., Bragg, R., Catlin, P. and Carlier, J. (1999) 'Do users want telecare and can it be cost-effective?', Paper presented at the EMBS/BMES International Conference, Atlanta, USA.

Brownsell, S., Bradley, D., Bragg, R., Catlin, P. and Carlier, J. (2001) 'An attributable cost model for a telecare system using advanced community alarms', *Journal of Telemedicine and Telecare*, vol 7, no 2, pp 63-72.

CallCentre Europe (1998) 'NHS Direct means health advice is just a phone call away', *CallCentre Europe*, vol 17, p 20.

Canter, R. (2001) 'Patients and medical power', *British Medical Journal* (www.bmj.com/cgi/content/full/323/7310/414), vol 323, p 414.

Celler, B.G., Earnshaw, W., Ilsar, E.D., Betbeder-Matibet, L., Harris, M.F., Clark, R., Hesketh, T. and Lovell, N.H. (1995) 'Remote monitoring of health status of the elderly at home: a multidisciplinary project on aging at the University of New South Wales', *International Journal of Biomedical Computing*, vol 40, no 2, pp 147-55.

Census and Government Actuary Data (1992) London: HMSO.

Cummings, S.R., Nevitt, M.C., Kidd, S. and Black, D. (1989) 'Risk factors for recurrent non-syncopal falls: a prospective study', *Journal of the American Medical Association*, vol 12, no 261, pp 2663-8.

Curry, R.G. and Norris, A.C. (1997) *A review and assessment of telecare activity in the UK and recommendations for development*, Southampton: New College, University of Southampton.

Despeignes, P. (2000) 'Smart homes aren't too far in the future', *The Detroit News* (http://detnews.com/specialreports/2000/technology/smart/smart.htm), 30 January.

DETR (Department of the Environment, Transport and the Regions) (2001) 'Supporting People: identifying support service costs and the amount of pooled rent income financing support services: draft' (www.housing.dtlr.gov.uk/information/la-guidance/pdf/draft-guidance.pdf).

DHSS (Department of Health and Social Security) (1978) *A happier old age: A discussion document*, London: HMSO.

Dixon, P. (1999) *Futurewise: Six faces of global change*, London: Harper Collins.

DoH (Department of Health) (1991) 'The National Service Framework for Older people' (www.doh.gov.uk/nsf/frameup/1.html).

DoH (1992) *Long-term care for elderly people: Purchasing, providing and quality*, London: HMSO.

DoH (1996) *Commons Health Committee*, London: HMSO.

DoH (1997) *The new NHS: Modern, dependable*, Cmd 3807, London: The Stationery Office.

DoH *Statistical Bulletin* (1998) 'Community care statistics 1998', table A1.2 (Households receiving home care or home care, by sector and age)' (see www.ace.org.uk).

DoH (1998a) 'Supplementary information on the ICT research initiative' (www.doh.gov.uk/ict.htm), p 6.

DoH (1998b) *Modernising social services: Promoting independence, improving protection, raising standards*, White Paper, London: DoH.

DoH (1999a) *Promoting independence: Partnership, prevention and carers – Conditions and allocations 1999/2000*, LAC (99) 13, London: DoH.

DoH (1999b) *Saving lives: Our healthier nation*, White Paper, London: DoH.

DoH (2000a) *The NHS Plan* (www.doh.gov.uk/ nhsplan/npch1.htm).

DoH (2000b) '£5.8m for on-line patient records' (http://213.38.88.196/coi/coipress.nsf), 19 June.

DoH (2001a) 'Building the information core: implementing the NHS Plan' (www.doh.gov.uk/ ipu/strategy/overview/overview.pdf).

DoH (2001b) 'The National Service Framework for Older People' (www.doh.gov.uk/nsf/olderpeople).

DoH (2001c) 'Guide to integrating community equipment services' (www.doh.gov.uk/pdfs/ cesguidance.pdf).

DoH (2002) 'Delivering 21st century IT support for the NHS' (www.doh.gov.uk/ipu/whatnew/ deliveringit/nhsitimpplan.pdf).

Doughty, K. and Cameron, K. (1996) *The role of electronic sensors in future telecare systems*, Bangor: University of Wales, Bangor.

Doughty, K., Cameron, K.H. and Matthews, M. (1995) 'The virtual neighbourhood', *Geriatric Medicine*, vol 25, pp 18-19.

Doughty, K., Cameron, K. and Garner, P. (1996) 'Three generations of telecare of the elderly', *Journal of Telemedicine and Telecare*, vol 2, pp 71-80.

Down, D. (ed) (2002) *Family spending: A report on the 2000-2001 Family Expenditure Survey*, London: The Stationery Office.

Drury, C. (1994) *Management and cost accounting*, London: Chapman & Hall, p 237.

DTI (Department of Trade and Industry) (2000) *Health care 2020*, London: DTI.

DTLR (Department for Transport, Local Government and the Regions) (1998) *Modernising local government: In touch with the people*, White Paper, London: DTLR.

DTLR (2000) *Quality and choice: A decent home for all*, Housing Green Paper, London: DTLR.

DTLR (2001) *Community alarm services: Reviewing and making judgements: Forthcoming guidance on Supporting People*, London: DTLR.

DTLR/DoH (2001) *Quality and choice for older people's housing: A strategic framework* (www.housing.odpm.gov.uk/information/hsc/ olderpeople).

Dyer, S., Clark, H. and Hartman, L. (1996) *Going home: Older people leaving hospital*, Bristol/York: The Policy Press/Joseph Rowntree Foundation.

Edinvar Housing Association (2000) 'AID house: assisted interactive dwelling – house', Publicity leaflet.

Electronic Telegraph (1997) 'GPs' house calls go virtual', 28 January, p 613.

Ermisch, J. (1990) *Fewer babies longer lives*, York: Joseph Rowntree Foundation.

Eurolink Centre for International Research (1992) *Eurolink Age Bulletin*, November.

Fisk, M. (1996) *Telecare equipment in the home: Issues of intrusiveness and control*, London: TeleMed 96.

Fisk, M. (1998) 'Telecare at home: factors influencing technology choices and user acceptance', *Journal of Telemedicine and Telecare*, vol 4, no 5, pp 80-3.

Gann, D., Burley, R., Curry, D., Phippen, P., Porteus, J., Wells, O. and Williams, M. (2000) *Healthcare and smart housing technologies: Report of a DTI international technology services mission to Japan*, Brighton: Pavilion.

Gavigan, J., Ottisch, M. and Greaves, C. (1999) *Demographic and social trends: Panel Report for the Futures Project*, EUR 18729EN (ftp://ftp.jrc.es/put/EURdoc/eur18729en.pdf).

Godfrey, M. (1999) *Preventive strategies for older people: Mapping the literature on effectiveness and outcomes*, Oxford: Anchor Research.

Goldring, M. (1998) 'Goldring: the age of rationing', Channel 4, 28 June.

Government Statistical Service (1996) *DoH Statistical Bulletin community care statistics 1995: Personal social services: Day and domiciliary services for adults England*, London: DoH.

Green, H. (1988) *Informal carers, General Household Survey 1985 series*, General Household Survey No 15, Supplement 16, London: OPCS, Social Survey Division.

Griffiths, D. (1996) *Politics of health*, Pulse Publications, p 67.

Grundy, E. (1998) 'Ageing, ill health and disability', in R. Tallis (ed) *Increasing longevity: Medical, social and political implications*, London: Royal College of Physicians of London.

Hagan, K., Hillman, M., Hanan, S. and Jepson, J. (1997) 'The design of a wheelchair mounted robot', IEE Computing and Control Division – Computers in the service of mankind: helping the disabled, *IEE Colloquium (Digest)*, no 117.

Health Care Research, Harris Heritage (2001) 'The increasing impact of eHealth on physician behaviour', (www.harrisinteractive.com/news/newsletters/healthnews/HI_HealthCareNews2001Vol1_iss31.pdf).

Health Select Committee (2002) 'Health – Third Report' (www.publications.parliament.uk/pa/cm200102/cmselect/cmhealth/617/61702.htm), 24 July.

Hyer, K. and Rudick, L. (1994) 'The effectiveness of personal emergency response systems in meeting the safety monitoring needs of home care clients', *Journal of Nursing Administration*, vol 24, no 6, pp 39-44.

Iakovidis, I. and Balas, E.A. (1999) 'Distance technologies for patient monitoring', *British Medical Journal*, vol 319, p 1309.

Joseph Rowntree Foundation (1998) 'Smart moves', *Search*, vol 31, pp 14-15.

Knipscheer, K. (1994) *Elderly, elderly disabled and technology*, Brussels: Gummerus Printing.

Lindberg, C.C. (1997) 'Implementation of in-home telemedicine in rural Kansas: answering an elderly patients needs', *Journal of American Medicine Association*, vol 4, no 1, pp 14-17.

Living in Retirement (2000) 'Safe and secure', p 6.

Loeb, G.E. (1999) 'Telecare: enabling the virtual housecall' (www.hctr.be.cua.edu/HCTworkshop/HCT-pos_GL-telecare.htm).

Mair, F.S., Haycox, A., May, C. and Williams, T. (2000) 'A review of telemedicine cost-effectiveness studies', *Journal of Telemedicine and Telecare*, vol 6, no 1, pp 38-40.

Martin, J. and Roberts, J. (1984) *Women in employment: A lifetime perspective*, London: HMSO.

Miyazaki, S. (1997) 'Long-term unrestrained measurement of stride length and walking velocity utilising a piezoelectric gyroscope', *IEEE Transactions on Biomedical Engineering*, vol 44, no 8, pp 753-9.

Murray, I. (1998) 'NHS will get £250m to end winter crises', *The Times*, 4 November.

Myers, G. and Coltrane, L. (1993) 'Social implications of ageing in developing countries', in *Short term training in the demographic aspects of population ageing and its implications for socio-economic development policies and plans*, Malta: International Institute on Ageing, United Nations.

NHIMAC (National Health Information Management Advisory Council) (2001) 'Health online: a health information action plan for Australia' (2nd edn) (www.health.gov.au/healthonline/actionp_2.pdf).

NHS Executive (1998) 'Information for health: an information strategy for the modern NHS 1998-2005' (www.doh.gov.uk/ipu/strategy/full/imt.pdf).

O'Cathain, A., Munro, J.F., Nicholl, P. and Knowles, E. (2000) 'How helpful is NHS Direct? Postal survey of callers', *British Medical Journal* (http://bmj.com/cgi/content/full/320/7241/1035).

ONS (Office for National Statistics) (1997) *Living in Britain: Results from the 1995 General Household Survey*, London: The Stationery Office.

OPCS (Office for Population Censuses and Surveys) (1994) *1992 General Household Survey*, London: HMSO.

OPCS (1996) *Living in Britain: Results from the 1994 General Household Survey*, London: The Stationery Office.

Palmore, E.B. and Burchett, B.M. (1997) 'Predictors of disability in the final year of life', *Journal of Ageing and Health*, vol 9, no 3, pp 282-97.

Parry, I. and Thompson, L. (1993) *Effective sheltered housing: A handbook*, London: Longman/Institute of Housing, p 12.

Porteus, J. and Brownsell, S. (2000) *Using telecare: Exploring technologies for independent living for older people*, Oxford: Anchor Research.

Prophet, H. (1998a) *From consumerism to citizenship: New European perspectives on independent living in older age*, Oxford: HOPE (Housing for Older People in Europe).

Prophet, H. (1998b) *Fit for the future: The future for public services – 2008*, London.

Randall, B. (2000) 'Net gains', *Housing*, July and August, pp 40-1.

Ranger, S. (2002) 'NHS spending on IT will top £1bn in 2002', *Computing*, p 1.

RCLTC (Royal Commission on Long-Term Care) (1999) *With respect to old age: Long term care – Rights and responsibilities*, London: The Stationery Office.

Research into Ageing (1997) 'Focus on healthy ageing: Dementia', Leaflet Number 1, London: Research into Ageing.

Research into Ageing (1998) 'Healthy ageing: news, views and research', London: Research into Ageing.

Richardson, S. (1993) 'Mobility and falls in the elderly', *The Canadian Journal of Geriatrics*, vol 9, no 5, pp 17-24.

Riseborough, M. (1997) *Community alarm services today and tomorrow*, Oxford: Anchor Research.

Roth, A., Carthy, Z. and Benedek, M. (1997) 'Telemedicine in emergency home care – the "Shahal" experience', *Journal of Telemedicine and Telecare*, vol 3, no 1, pp 58-60.

Roth, A., Malov, N., Carthy, Z., Golovner, M., Naveh, R., Alroy, I., Kaplinsky, E. and Laniado, S. (2000) 'Potential reduction of cost and hospital emergency department visit resulting from pre-hospital transtelephonic triage: the "SHAHAL" experience in Israel', *Clinical Cardiology*, vol 23, pp 271-6.

Roush, R.E., Teasdale, T.A., Murphy, J.N. and Kirk, M.S. (1995) 'Impact of a personal emergency response system on hospital utilisation by community residing elders', *South Medical Journal*, vol 88, no 9, pp 917-22.

Rudel, D., Premik, M. and Hojnik-Zupanc, I. (1995) 'Caring network based on community social alarm centres in Slovenia: a country in transition', *MedInfo*, vol 8, no 2, pp 1503-5.

Smit, J. (1997) 'Open house', *Building Homes*, no 10.

Smith, R. (2001) 'Almost no evidence exists that the internet harms health', *British Medical Journal*, 22 September (http://bmj.com/cgi/content/full/323/7314/651/b), vol 323, p 651.

Tang, P., Gann, D. and Curry, R. (2000) *Telecare: New ideas for care and support @ home*, Bristol: The Policy Press.

The Times (1997) 'Fingertip chips can reveal all to doctors', 21 May.

Thornton, P. and Moutain, G. (1992) 'Please ring for service', *Community Care*, vol 11, pp 20-1.

Tinker, A. (1997) *Older people in modern society*, Harlow: Longman.

Tunstall Telecom (1997) *Home alone 97: Independence and isolation*, Tunstall Telecom.

Turner-Smith, A. (2000) 'Help required: what is assistive technology?', *The Newsletter of the Centre of Rehabilitation Engineering*, Review 17, Spring, p 5.

Wallace, S., Wyatt, J. and Taylor, P. (1998) 'Telemedicine in the NHS for the millennium and beyond', *Journal of Postgraduate Medicine*, vol 74, pp 721-8.

Wanless, D. (2001) 'Securing our future health: taking a long-term view' (www.hm-treasury.gov.uk/Consultations_and_Legislation/wanless/consult_wanless_index).

Warnes, A. (1993) *The demography of ageing in the United Kingdom of Great Britain and Northern Ireland*, London: Age Concern Institute of Gerontology and the Department of Geography, Kings College, University of London.

Watts, L. and Monk, A. (1997) *Telemedical consultation: Task characteristics* (www.acm.org/sigs/sigchi/chi97/proceedings/tech-note/law.htm), p 534.

Wenger, C. (1993) 'The ageing world, longevity, culture and the individual', *Generations Review*, vol 3, no 3, p 4, September.

Whipple, R., Wolfson, L.I., Amerman, P. and Tobin, J.N. (1990) 'Gait assessment in the elderly: a gait abnormality rating scale and its relation to falls', *Journal of Gerontology*, vol 45, pp 12-19.

Whitten, P., Mair, F. and Collins, B. (1997) 'Home telenursing in Kansas: patients' perceptions of uses and benefits', *Journal of Telemedicine and Telecare*, vol 3, no 1, pp 67-9.

Williams, G., Brownsell, S., Bradley, D., Bragg, R., Catlin, P. and Carlier, J. (1999) 'Future systems for remote health care', *Journal of Telemedicine and Telecare*, vol 5, pp 141-52.

Wootton, R., Loane, M., Mair, F., Allen, A., Doolittle, G., Begley, M., Mclernan, A., Moutray, M. and Harrison, S. (1998) 'A joint US–UK study of home telenursing', *Journal of Telemedicine and Telecare*, vol 4, no 1, pp 83-5.

Wright, D. (1998a) 'Telemedicine and developing countries', *Journal of Telemedicine and Telecare*, vol 4, no 2, pp 1-87.

Wright, D. (1998b) 'Appendix 1: telemedicine experience', *Journal of Telemedicine and Telecare*, vol 4, no 2, pp 49-61.

Appendix: Standard questionnaire

FLAT NUMBER _____

1. Male/female _____

2. Live alone/couple _____

3. Do you like having a community alarm and are you satisfied with it?

Yes, definitely ☐
Mainly yes ☐
No, not really ☐
No ☐

4. Do you currently have a pendant?

Yes ☐
No ☐

5. Number of pull cords tied up/not wearing pendant?

Not wearing pendant ☐
Number of inoperable pull cords ☐
Which rooms _____

6. Given the choice would you rather have:

Just pendant ☐
Pendant and 1 pull cord ☐
Pendant and all pull cords ☐
Just pull cords ☐

7. Which pendant do you prefer?

Wrist ☐
Brooch ☐
Neck cord ☐

8. Would you like to be able to answer the telephone by the pendant and speak into the pendant, for telephone calls and the door entry system?

Yes ☐
Perhaps ☐
No ☐

9. Would you prefer the main community alarm unit:

As it is ☐
Built into telephone ☐
As a clock on the wall ☐
    Analogue ☐
    Digital ☐

10. In the last year how many times have you used the alarm unit? _____

11. In the last year how many times have you wanted to raise an alarm for help but have been unable to do so? _____

12. In these examples would you contact the warden/control centre or contact the people directly yourself?

Fire ☐
Ambulance ☐
Police ☐
GP ☐
Repairs ☐

13. Would you allow a sensor to be placed in each room that could trace your movements, so unusual behaviour, such as you being in the living room but not moving, for, say 5 hours, raised an alarm?

Yes, definitely ☐
Yes, probably ☐
Probably not ☐
No ☐
Don't know ☐
If unit was smaller ☐

14. Would you allow the sensor to be installed in the bathroom?

Yes, definitely ☐
Yes, probably ☐
Probably not ☐
No ☐
Don't know ☐
If unit was smaller ☐

15. If an alarm were raised the alarm unit could automatically speak to you with a recorded message. You could respond to this by moving or pressing your pendant and this would cancel the call. Alternatively if you didn't respond the warden/control centre would be called. Would you like this automatic speech message before the unit called the warden/control centre?

Yes ☐
No ☐
Perhaps ☐
Don't know ☐

16. Would you like to have a small medical unit, that your doctor would set up for you, and when you used it, perhaps once a week, it would check your health and inform you?

Yes ☐
No ☐
Perhaps ☐
If doctor decided ☐

17. If you were to fall over and were unable to get up would you like this to be automatically detected and the warden or control centre contacted?

Yes ☐
No ☐
Perhaps ☐
Don't know ☐

18. Would you be prepared for the health information to be kept so the doctor can use this when you next need their help?

Yes ☐
No ☐
If GP thought wise ☐
Don't know ☐

19. Would you be prepared for information on when you have fallen to be kept so the doctor can use this when you next need their help?

Yes ☐
No ☐
If GP thought wise ☐
Don't know ☐

20. Would you be prepared for information on any unusual behaviour the system detected to be kept so the doctor can use this when you next need their help?

Yes ☐
No ☐
If GP thought wise ☐
Don't know ☐

21. Are you concerned about you or others leaving the gas on by mistake?

Very concerned ☐
Concerned ☐
Not concerned ☐
Indifferent ☐

22. In a normal week how often do you ring people, including the warden, on the scheme? _____

23. If this call was free how often do you think you would ring people on the scheme?

_____

24. When communicating with the warden, control centre or GP, as well as speaking to them through the alarm unit would you like to be able to see them on the television? (also other residents on the scheme)

Yes, all of the time ☐
Yes, most cases ☐
In some cases ☐
Not really ☐
No ☐

25. Would you like these people to be able to see you on their televisions?

Yes, definitely ☐
Probably ☐
No ☐
Don't know ☐

26. During a normal night how many times would you get up? _____

27. Would it help if when you got out of bed all the rooms that you went into automatically turned the lights on and off for you?

Yes, definitely ☐
Yes, most cases ☐
Perhaps ☐
No, not really ☐

28. Have you fallen over in the home during the last year? If yes, how many times? _____

29. How many times have you been to the doctors' surgery in the last year? _____

30. How many times has the doctor come to your home in the last year? _____

31. Have you been admitted to hospital in the last year? If yes, how many times? _____

32. Do you have any home care support? Number of hours per week? _____

33. Do you have any nursing support? Number of hours per week? _____

34. Does anyone else provide any support?
Number of hours per week? _____
Person for providing support? _____

35. Do you take any prescription tablets daily? If yes, how many? _____

36. How many times a day do you take the prescription drugs? _____

37. Do you sometimes forget to take your medication? If yes, how many times a month? _____

38. In general would you say your health is?

Excellent ❑
Very good ❑
Good ❑
Fair ❑
Poor ❑

39. When you activate the alarm how satisfied are you with the time it takes the warden to answer?

Always satisfied ❑
Normally satisfied ❑
Occasionally satisfied ❑
Sometimes dissatisfied ❑
Always dissatisfied ❑

40. When you activate the alarm how satisfied are you with the time it takes the control centre to answer?

Always satisfied ❑
Normally satisfied ❑
Occasionally satisfied ❑
Sometimes dissatisfied ❑
Always dissatisfied ❑

41. How many times a week do you go outside the scheme? _____

42. How often do friends visit you? _____

43. How often do relatives visit you? _____

44. Can you use?

Cooker ❑
Microwave ❑
Washing machine ❑
Vacuum cleaner ❑
Telephone ❑
Radio ❑
TV ❑
Video ❑
Computer ❑

1 - without help, quite easily
2 - without help but some difficulty
3 - with some help
4 - with a lot of help
5 - unable
N/A don't have that device

45. If you were advised to move into residential care or could stay here with technology, automatically detecting unusual behaviour, more community care and adaptations to the home would you prefer?

To stay here ❑
Move into care ❑

46. If an exercise class were available here for free would you attend?

Yes, definitely ❑
Yes, probably ❑
Might ❑
No ❑

47. Interviewee's age? _____